Hope you like looking at Photographs!

Happy Christmas 1988.

Ahse + Rou xx.

Queen Elizabeth
THE
QUEEN MOTHER

Foreword by Lord Howard de Walden
Text and captions by Trevor Hall

Editor
Bron Kowal

Editorial Director
David Gibbon

Designer
Sara Cooper

Production Director
Gerald Hughes

Publishing Director
Ted Smart

ACKNOWLEDGEMENTS
The publishers would like to thank Her Majesty the Queen for her gracious permission to reproduce photographs from Queen Mary's personal albums and other photographs in the Royal Collection, and to acknowledge the help given by Miss Frances Dimond, Curator of the Royal Photographic Collection at Windsor Castle. The publishers also wish to express their gratitude to Her Royal Highness Princess Alice, Duchess of Gloucester for the loan of a photograph from her private albums, to the Earl and Countess of Strathmore and Kinghorne for permission to reproduce photographs in their possession at Glamis, and to the Hon Lady Bowes Lyon and the St Paul's Walden Charities for assistance and permissions to use photographs from family albums. The publishers further acknowledge with gratitude the help given to the author by Major John Griffin at Clarence House and Col. David Lloyd-Jones, recently retired Administrator of the Strathmore Estates.

Photographic acknowledgements
Reproduced by gracious permission of HM Queen Elizabeth II: all photographs on pages 13, 22-25, 29, 31-35, 37, 38, 46, 48-51, 53, 54, 56, 57, 59-61, 88, 91, 111, 116, 119, 128-131, 144-146; also 90 (top) and 92 (bottom left).
The property of HRH Princess Alice, Duchess of Gloucester: page 176 (bottom left).
The property of the Earl and Countess of Strathmore and Kinghorne: pages 21 and 87.
The property of St Paul's Walden Charities: all photographs on pages 15-18, 20, 26 and 27.

CLB 1873
First published in Great Britain 1987.
Copyright © 1987 Text: Colour Library Books Ltd., Guildford, Surrey, England.
Copyright © 1987 Illustrations: Photo Source, London, and Colour Library Books, except as acknowledged above.
Printed and bound in Barcelona, Spain by Cronion S.A.

ISBN 0 86283 568 2

Queen Elizabeth
THE
QUEEN MOTHER

Text by
Trevor Hall

Foreword by
Lord Howard de Walden

COLOUR LIBRARY BOOKS

Foreword
by Lord Howard de Walden

To be asked to write a foreword to a book about the life of Queen Elizabeth the Queen Mother is an honour indeed. The hundreds of photographs in this magnificent volume not only illustrate Queen Elizabeth's long and varied life, but also explain why she is surely the most beloved person in this country, and in many other countries beyond the seas.

Queen Elizabeth is known to have a multitude of interests, among which is horse-racing – or in her case steeplechasing. She loves her horses, and enjoys the whole atmosphere that goes with the racecourse. I remember one occasion when our horses were in opposition and it was more than probable that one of us would win. The trophy was a whole service of china, and as we walked together to look at it, Queen Elizabeth said quietly to me, "I wonder which of us needs this the least!"

Her sense of fun and enjoyment is infectious, and her apparently endless reserve of energy is illustrated by the occasion when a mutual friend took her out to dinner, and I was fortunate enough to be one of the party. It was a summer evening and quite late when we all returned to Clarence House, but Queen Elizabeth immediately suggested we all play croquet – and so we did, amid much laughter, till well after midnight.

I am sure the photographs in this book will bring all its readers warmth and happiness, as Queen Elizabeth has done over the years, and that they will stir memories of her courage and the lead she gave the nation in the dark days of the War.

Queen Elizabeth has had the good fortune to combine her royal position with a real link with ordinary people and their personal lives. This is a gift of the highest order. May she long enjoy many more birthdays to lighten our hearts, and continue to show us all that life is a great adventure and one to be enjoyed.

Howard de Walden.

Hers is a story which it is becoming increasingly difficult not to begin with the words, "Once upon a time...". Looking back across nine decades to its relatively quiet, uncomplicated beginnings in the bosom of a large, close family lends it a glow which is perhaps the prerogative of all life stories that sprang into existence in the half-forgotten world of the very last Victorians.

She is, in strict truth, a Victorian herself, born less than six months before the last reigning Queen-Empress took her dying breath. Equally strictly, she was a 19th-century baby, since that century had five months to run before giving way to the twentieth on 1st January, 1901. But these are academic identifications. She has belonged exclusively to no one age, neither pre-War nor post-War, neither Edwardian, Georgian nor Elizabethan. She has belonged to them all; has lived, experienced and, in her way, served them all to such an extent that her story is very much the story of the twentieth century.

Perversely, it began with a little white lie. Today, in exchange for a crisp, blue five-pound note bearing the image of her daughter, you can buy a copy of her birth certificate, which will tell you that she was born on 4th August, 1900 at St Paul's Walden Bury. The date is right, the place wrong. She was in fact born at 20 St James's Square, where her parents, Lord and Lady Glamis, lived during their business and social sojourns in London. The explanation of the discrepancy varies depending upon whom you ask, but it seems common ground that Lady Glamis' impending confinement kept both her and her husband in the hot, airless capital far longer than they would have liked after the end of the Season the previous month. Both were desperate to remove to their Queen Anne mansion at St Paul's Walden, in the rolling Hertfordshire countryside, and as soon as mother and baby were ready for the journey, off they all went. In the aftermath of their arrival, the constant stream of congratulating visitors and the general atmosphere of leisure-taking discouraged Lord Glamis from doing anything about registering the birth. In events, he overran the statutory six-week period of grace, and on reporting at last to the Registrar at nearby Hitchin, was fined the princely sum of seven shillings and sixpence. Presuming it as well to be hanged for a sheep as for a lamb, he then innocuously falsified the place of birth, preferring that his newly-born daughter should be believed to have first seen the light of day in his wonderful old family freehold property, rather than in some leasehold London town house that no Strathmore would ever own.

It was not as if he was inexperienced in these matters, though it was admittedly seven years since the Glamises' last child was born. Elizabeth Angela Marguerite, as the new baby was named, was the ninth of their children to be born in the nineteen years since they married. Sadly, the eldest of her siblings had already died at the age of 11, but even so the senior of the seven remaining was about to celebrate her seventeenth birthday. So it was a huge family that Elizabeth joined, and there was, no

doubt, ample opportunity for indulgence from parents, brothers and sisters. But not for long. Elizabeth was only twenty-one months old when along came the tenth and last child. He was christened David, was adored by his elder sister, became her constant companion in childhood, and her favourite brother for life. Within the family, the two of them carved out their own interlocking and inseparable relationship, and were endearingly known as the two Benjamins.

They came to love life at St Paul's, with its woods and wide open spaces, its statues and hedge-lined allees, its huge rocking horses and the great chart on the wall of the hall where successive generations of children had recorded their growing height from year to year. It's still there today, and Elizabeth's name is hidden among those of her brothers, sisters, cousins and other more recent relatives. No less did they adore the fresher climes and more romantic ambiance of Glamis Castle, nestling in the hills just south of the Grampians, with its echoing stone crypt and armoury, its ghost-haunted chapel with its strange painting of Christ with a hat on, its endless staircases where the muted, sinister ticking of the tower clock sounded, and its huge, lofty reception rooms where floorboards creaked and proud, frowning ancestors gazed down. Here was a beautiful Italian garden, a dovecot alive with hundreds of pigeons, dark woodland walks, and such castellated walls and turrets that there was always somewhere new to stage a mock battle. And here too was that wonderful old chest packed full of old costumes that made dressing-up a regular must.

For most of us, childhood merges imperceptibly into adolescence, which in turn merges into adulthood. For Lady Elizabeth (as she became in 1904 when her father inherited the title Earl of Strathmore), there was no such luxury. The long Edwardian postlude to Victorian peace and stability came to an abrupt end when, on her fourteenth birthday, Britain declared war on Germany and her allies. Elizabeth was at the theatre at the time, leaving at the end of the show to make her way through streets choking with noisy, enthusiastic, innocently patriotic people whose only wish was to fete volunteers and acclaim their Sovereign at Buckingham Palace. Had she known that she herself would appear on that same balcony during the prelude to another, more terrible war, she would have been horrified. As it was, she shared with the rest the naive belief that it would all end Britain's way by Christmas.

But there was no magic in Christmas when it came. Instead, it saw the conversion of parts of her beloved Glamis into a convalescent ward, and the arrival of an endless stream of wounded soldiers at the rate of some four hundred a year. And interminable years they were, too, for in their course her brother Fergus was killed, the two eldest were wounded, and a fourth taken prisoner. One of her uncles was also killed, along with three cousins, and another two cousins were ferried back to Britain with severe wounds. But it's an ill wind that blows nobody any good, and those four long years established Elizabeth as a budding charmer, quiet, modest and efficient, with the will to care for her charges and a flair for making them as welcome at Glamis as members of her own family. She served their meals, fetched their cigarettes, helped write their letters, played cards with them and generally gave them the will to make light of their misfortunes and forget the slaughter from which they had returned.

In events, it was an apt apprenticeship for the novel, uncertain and questioning world of peace, reconstruction and social change. When she was finally launched into Society, she was an instant success, showing all the traditional accomplishments, and untarnished by the wildness that was later to mark out the debutante from the flapper. She was widely known as one of the best dancers in town, and before long was hosting house-parties at Glamis, where acquaintances with the Royal Family were quietly cultivated. And it was through her close friendship with the King's daughter, Princess Mary, whose bridesmaid she became in 1922, that a more persistent association began with Prince Albert, Duke of York.

Prince Albert - "Bertie" to family and friends - was last of all a socialite. For all the luxury and creature comforts of the Court in which he lived and moved, he suffered a loveless childhood, a rigorous adolescence and a timorous release into manhood. He was scared witless of his often querulous father, and found little comfort in the company of his mother, Queen Mary, to whom affection was very much a closed book. He had pursued a reluctant career in the Navy, which in 1918 he forsook for the Royal Flying Corps. Though the latter offered him the occasional opportunity to escape from the vacuous shibboleths of Court life, there can be little doubt that despite his appreciation of his public calling, he yearned for his own small, quiet family life. In Lady Elizabeth Bowes Lyon he found, at the first attempt, the key to this modest ambition.

The trouble was that the lady was not ready to help him realise it. It may be the dream of many to marry into a truly royal existence, though it is not, as far as we know, every day that one is proposed to by a member of the Royal Family. It was certainly a measure of Elizabeth's independence of spirit and clarity of vision that she refused Bertie at the first time of asking. The explanations she left to her mother - a feeling that she was unworthy of such a potentially high calling, and an unease about giving up a very private life for a very public one. By contrast, it was equally a measure of Bertie's unexpected singularity of purpose that he refused to take No for an answer. Following a decent interval, he was back at Glamis, resuming his quest for the lady whom he was determined to make his bride.

By January 1923 he had succeeded. A quiet walk in the grounds of St Paul's Walden, while the rest of the Strathmores were at church, ended with a proposal that was accepted. Bertie telegraphed his parents at Sandringham immediately, and it seems that at that moment they finally accepted him for the mature and responsible young man he was. The King found himself utterly taken with his prospective daughter-in-law, and enthused constantly about her charm. Queen Mary, equally bowled over, wrote affectionate letters to Lady Strathmore and peppered her voluminous journal with cosy references to "Bertie & E." The young couple were in a world of their own, slightly bemused by all the fuss, and expressing mock horror as the press seized upon the news. "I fear the cat is completely out of the bag," Elizabeth wrote to a friend, "and there is no way of stuffing him back in again."

Long before her daughter became engaged, Lady Strathmore had described Bertie as a man who would be made or marred by his wife, and events following upon the momentous glow of the Yorks' wedding in April 1923 showed her to be right. Within four years Elizabeth had persuaded Bertie to take steps to alleviate a speech impediment that made public speaking a persistent nightmare, had smoothed over relationships between him and his parents, and had built up a confidence in him which was never there before - to the point where, when she fell ill during their Australasian tour of 1927, he wondered whether he should not cancel his own engagements as well as hers. And in 1926, she presented him with their first child. The lady we now know as Elizabeth II began life as the fair-haired baby girl who, Bertie himself confessed, now made his happiness complete.

Almost a quarter of a century later he was, as King, to divulge to his people that but for the inner strength he derived from a happy family life, he would have found it impossible to sustain the burden of kingship which ten hectic years had placed upon him. Much has indeed been made of the part played by his wife in the domestic, national and international events that were soon radically to reshape the world - a role which has frequently been so overstated as almost to imply the preposterous conclusions that she saved the monarchy from the jaws of oblivion, personally sealed Britain's international alliances, and won the war virtually single-handed. A more detached view must put firmly in its place the real function and purpose of monarchy as a primarily social force with limited political influences, yet it cannot be denied that as a national and occasionally international focal point it attracts more than its fair share of pressure. And after a blissful, almost undisturbed decade of serene and fulfilled married life, the Yorks were soon to realise how fierce that pressure would be. At the same time, Elizabeth was to discover, if she had ever had doubts on the subject, how indispensable she would become to her earnest, conscientious husband whose tendency was to submit to outside pressures rather than resist them.

By the time of King George V's Silver Jubilee in 1935, Elizabeth had acquired a pleasant, if somewhat saccharine, reputation as the perfect wife and mother, a woman of many talents and disciplines who combined an assiduous attitude to her public duties with a personal responsibility for the upbringing and welfare of her two delightful daughters, and her role as a homemaker to their busy father. Public tittle-tattle spoke nothing, however, of the sheer steel which lay beneath her gracious, smiling appearance, and which drove her to strive for the best in everything she undertook, and to suffer no fool or adversary too gladly. Although she had made herself very much at home as a member of the Royal Family, accepting its sometimes faintly amusing traditions and stuffiness as easily as finding her own innovative self accepted, she was not without discrimination. So it was that, when in the early months of the new reign of King Edward VIII, she was first introduced to Mrs Ernest Simpson, upon whom the eyes of the whole of London society had been cast for two or three rivetting years, she made it clear that, to quote Mrs Simpson herself, "she was not sold on the King's American interest."

The story of the Abdication has been told many times, and from the point of view of everyone from malicious gossipers to serious historians, and from partisans to the main protagonists themselves. Barring the occasional reported quote, however, there is little hard, first-hand evidence of the attitude taken then and since by the lady who became Queen Consort in its aftermath. What does seem to be clear, however, is that she was appalled by the cavalier way in which her brother-in-law ditched his public duties to pursue his courtship of Mrs Simpson, made no effort to conceal his social indiscretions from an increasingly avid press, and, worst of all, kept his own wilful counsel to the virtual exclusion of his staff, his ministers and his family. She was agonisingly aware that Queen Mary's rigid sense of public duty was being progressively outraged by her son's thoughtlessness, and she sympathised with the utter bewilderment and shock that gradually overtook the ageing and recently widowed Queen. And she was furious that her first intimation of the breaking of the crisis came, not through any communication from the King himself, but by way of a newspaper bill-board which she spotted on emerging from King's Cross Station after a journey to London from Edinburgh.

Her increasing indignation probably owed most, however, to the plight of Bertie, knowing that his introspective nature and unwillingness to make any kind of a scene made it almost impossible for him to go onto the offensive in the frustrating quest for hard news from his brother whom, despite the striking contrasts in their personalities, he had always admired and implicitly trusted. She found his being kept in ignorance of the fate that awaited him both demeaning and despairing, and she deplored the vision of him, a man of forty, desperately blurting out to his Mountbatten cousin that he was totally unprepared for kingship, and sobbing like a child in the arms of his mother at the humiliation of it all. The subsequent succession of events was relentless and, to one who had always been wary of being swallowed up by public service, crushing. When the inevitable happened, she took it with bitter resignation. Like many who lived through it, she never forgot; unlike many, she found forgiveness elusive.

Much of what the Duke and Duchess of Windsor have regarded as the successive snubs delivered to them in their attempts at even partial rehabilitation was and is owed to Elizabeth's strict and intransigent attitude toward the treachery she and her husband had suffered. Both at the time and since, she has been credited with the insistence that the Windsors should not be allowed to take up permanent residence in Britain, nor be given any public job or position in the service of the Crown. The discontinuation of telephone calls between the exiled brother and his successor has also been attributed in part to her influence, as has the withholding from the Duke's bride, on the very eve of their marriage in June 1937 of the style Her Royal Highness. This, above all else, rankled with the Windsors at the time, and has rankled, time and time again, ever since. But despite periodic grumbles by Windsor supporters, the occasional use of the style by the Duke himself in private, a lengthy discourse by Debrett in favour of its granting, and the strong possibility that several members of the Royal Family - notably Princess Michael of Kent - would have preferred to see it happen, the courtesy was never accorded. So, for little short of fifty years, the old sore was left unhealed. And since both Duke and Duchess have passed away, it will remain unhealed for ever.

It says much for the psychological stamina of the new King and Queen that by the approach of their Coronation, five months after the hectic and disturbing days of the Abdication, Elizabeth was able to write freely that "the curious thing is that we are not afraid." Even some erstwhile Windsor supporters noted the Queen's growing confidence, and her obvious enjoyment of her new role, with surprised, if sometimes grudging satisfaction, while fast friends, clergy and Government ministers saw the royal couple's increasing presence and dignity reflected in an enormous surge of popularity. This popular acclaim, while focused on the quiet figure of the King, depended for its persistence on the more outgoing charm of his wife. In March 1937, the politician Harold Nicolson attended a royal dinner party and was amazed by the Queen's cool charm and dignity. "I cannot help feeling," he mused, "what a mess poor Mrs Simpson would have made of such an occasion. It demonstrated to us more than anything else how wholly impossible that marriage would have been."

Had she known of this diaried remark, Elizabeth would have valued it for the rest of her days, not just for its own complimentary sentiment but as an objective measure of the way she had come through a most unenviable experience. Certainly she built on her early progress. The Coronation lacked nothing in brilliance except weather; that glittering State Visit to France in 1938 took the French by storm and sent them into a spasm of regret for the monarchies they had discarded in the previous century; and an even more monumental tour of Canada in 1939 was topped with a superlative, if short, stay in Washington at the invitation of President Roosevelt. Accounts of all those highly newsworthy tours read as one in their high profile projection not so much of the King, but of the Queen.

Hers were the gestures they noticed, the words they savoured, the fashions they copied, the attentions they craved. She had, as the Canadian Governor-General put it, a perfect genius for the right kind of publicity; while King George was gratified in his modest way by the assurance from one American senator that he sure was a great Queen-picker!

If the three years since their accession had not already proved this to him, the immediate future would. As 1939's politically uncertain summer came to its end, Britain braced herself reluctantly and unbelievingly for war, amid a turmoil of conscription, evacuation, prospective privation and a frantic rush to plan and co-ordinate civil defence. The Royal Family, protected from the more immediate of the common man's problems, were however thrown into the urgent public business of war - the encouragement of factory production, the calming of fear and panic, the maintaining of loyalties, the endless speech-making, the continual visits to all parts of London and the big cities, all the stock-in-trade of boosting public morale. As a result of that unique role arose the dilemma as to whether to keep the two young princesses at risk in London for appearances' sake, or evacuate them to the country, along with so many other children, or even abroad. For the Queen there was no real choice: her family stayed together for the duration, and as the King would remain based in London, so would they all. Besides, as she told one of the King's ministers in 1940, personal patriotism was not consistent with defection, on whatever grounds. So it was that, while Britain welcomed royal families from all over Europe who sought refuge in these islands, or who were *en route* for quieter parts of the world, Britain's own royals matched their fate solidly with that of their nation: "We stay with our people."

It was not always an easy point to put over. Despite – perhaps in a perverse way, because of – the several visits the King and Queen made to the bombed areas of East and South London, at a time when only those underprivileged districts seemed to be alone in taking the worst of Hitler's bombs, a gradual antagonism against the Royal Family and its well-heeled acolytes manifested itself to the point where, unusually for almost any time this century, the King and Queen were being jeered in the streets. Personally distressed at the realisation that even royal sympathy and encouragement had limitations when received by despairing, deprived victims, the royal couple saw in this reaction the beginnings of popular discontent on a wider, more alarming scale. Whether this trend would have continued it is now academic to argue, but the bombing of Buckingham Palace must, for all the terror and vulnerability to which it exposed the first family, have been greeted with a measure of relief. Here, at last, was a veneer - and it may well have been nothing more than that - of common suffering between rulers and ruled. At least, the Queen thought so. "I'm glad we've been bombed," runs her most celebrated remark. "It makes me feel I can look the East End in the face."

Without doubt, she made the most of the few opportunities the war offered. She forged a strong and lasting friendship with Eleanor Roosevelt who came over to London to inspect women's war work and the activities of various American support groups. Hitherto no great enthusiast for making radio broadcasts, she found the wireless very much her medium, a discovery that was shared by millions, particularly among women, in Britain and abroad, to whom her messages were directed. She became a firm favourite with the Prime Minister of the day, the bulldog-spirited Winston Churchill who put traditional loyalties to the Crown before all else and who paid tribute to her unique wartime style with the words: "Many an aching heart found solace in her gracious smile." And she took a shine to what we now take for granted as the royal walkabout, as sheer force of chaotic circumstance in the midst of ruined communities and bombed areas rendered the usual royal formalities eminently dispensable. She ran weekly sewing circles at Buckingham Palace, made regular ventures out to listen to lunchtime recitals in London, and even took her own small part in the Buckingham Palace Home Guard training programme, learning how to work stirrup pumps, perfecting her gas-mask drill and being taught to handle and fire a revolver. Meanwhile, never one to forget that life could still be enjoyed by the young, she encouraged those famous Christmas pantomimes at Windsor, which for three consecutive years kept her daughters occupied and which nurtured Princess Margaret's already pronounced theatrical proclivities.

As with the First World War, she did not escape personal loss. Two of her Bowes Lyon nephews returned home wounded in action, while a third - the young heir to the Strathmore title - was killed; meanwhile the King's brother, the Duke of Kent died on active service in the Royal Air Force, when his aircraft crashed during a flight over Scotland. Tragic though these losses may have been, they were mere reflections of what ordinary people in far less enviable circumstances than the Royal Family had suffered rather more grievously in terms of personal bereavement and loss of homes and possessions. Yet it seemed that, as the tide of fortune turned in the last two years of the war, no tragedy was too great for the British to hold against the mystical focal point that was and is the monarchy. Just as the Queen had confidently commended the actions of her husband's subjects as so magnificent as to ensure victory in the long run, so the people of Britain turned to hail their King and Queen when victory finally arrived.

It was a short-lived rejoicing, followed as it was by the turmoil of a general election and change of government, by a quiet but significant socio-political upheaval, and by three or four long, hard years of austerity. But it was also a period which many of that generation still regard as the heyday of modern royalty, when the magic vision with which it was still popularly perceived graced joyless lives with a glow of richness, glamour, almost sanctity. 1947 was a typical year. At its beginning, Britain was in the grip of the sort of dreadful winter which stays in the record books for decades, and at the very nadir of post-war depression and economic helplessness. In those circumstances, it seemed almost cruel that the Royal Family should be sailing off to sunnier climes for a two-month visit to South Africa, yet not only was no voice raised against the tour, but its every move was watched and followed by an admiring British public who were rather proud to see their royal family flying the flag abroad. And while it was perhaps easy for the King to include in his speeches there a tactful reference to conditions at home, the sincerity of his anxieties was confirmed privately by the Queen in her letters to Queen Mary: "It is doubly hard for Bertie, who feels he should be at home. We think of home all the time."

During the tour, Princess Elizabeth came of age and made a famous speech of dedication to the service of her future peoples. Few knew at the time that she was concealing a yearning for the man she had already decided to marry - Prince Philip of Greece. Her engagement might well have been announced before the tour, but for her parents who advised that a timely and active absence would serve to give pause for final consideration. It was advice which they feared might well be resented by their daughter, though it is interesting to note that shortly before her wedding later that year, Princess Elizabeth wrote to her mother assuring her that it had been for the best. It was a November wedding, held on a bleakish day in the middle of an equally bleak, war-damaged London. But the day lives on in the memories of those who witnessed it as a pool of light and hope in the midst of austerity and struggle. In the sense that it projected the unspoken value of a benign and dutiful royal family even as social values were being recast, it was probably more memorable than the more colourful and magnificent royal weddings of recent years.

Princess Elizabeth's wedding, and the King and Queen's own silver wedding which followed five months later, proved the last bright flickers of the candle that marked the span of George VI's reign. Before 1948 was out the Queen was being advised that her husband was suffering severe circulatory problems and hardening of the arteries, and that he might even have to undergo the amputation of a leg to prevent gangrene. Circulation trouble recurred the following year, but was temporarily allayed by lumbar sympathectomy. His health never really recovered after that. A heavy smoker since his late teens, he developed influenza, and the inspection of an inflamed lung that followed revealed a cancerous growth. Despite the removal of the lung, the growth had already spread beyond medical powers of treatment. Less than a year after that operation, he was dead.

For the Queen those three years were probably the hardest of her life. Not only was she privy to much bad news that was best kept from her ailing husband, she also had to be selective about what to tell her elder daughter during her first pregnancy. In bad times, she had to be constantly at the King's side; in less bad times, she had to deputise for him in public in a way which gave no hint of the worsening prognosis. And all the time she had to come to terms herself with the inevitable she did not wish to face but could not avoid. Those now famous news pictures of the Royal Family at London Airport, seeing Princess Elizabeth off on a Commonwealth tour which she was, in events, unable to complete, illustrate perfectly the public and private dilemma - the Queen's habitual, cheery, somewhat fixed smile contrasting with the haunted, hollow features of the man whom Churchill described as walking with Death at his elbow.

Sandringham, which he loved and where he died, is also where his widow observes that sad anniversary each February. Though ceremonial guns are fired and flags are flown annually to celebrate her daughter's accession day, February 6th is a day for private thought and communing memories for the lady who chose thenceforth to be known as the Queen Mother. The early months of widowhood found her shattered and reclusive, unable or unwilling to ignite any spark of enthusiasm for even the most familiar of visitors. It took a secret arrangement between one of her ladies-in-waiting and Sir Winston Churchill – whereby Churchill was encouraged not to make an appointment to see her, but simply to turn up and explain to her, as only he could, how much she was missed and how much she could still contribute - to persuade her out of her withdrawal. Thus it was that, only months after the King died, she was back in the public eye, although dressed in deep mourning as if loyalties to the past made her uneasy about living the present.

But, though her years of widowhood have been, like Queen Victoria's, disproportionately long, the last thing the Queen Mother has been renowned for is her reluctance to live life to the full. Her move to Clarence House in 1953 gave her not only an official London base, but a very personal home which she proceeded to fill with favourite furnishings, tapestries and paintings, silver and glassware. Within a year she had spotted and decided to rescue from demolition the dilapidated old Barrogil Castle up on the north-east coast of Scotland, and a year later took up residence there. Now renamed the Castle of Mey, it is her place of annual pilgrimage, a home for three weeks in the year, and a quiet place close to Nature for herself, close family, and friends to enjoy. It was during this early period that she consolidated her newly-formed love of horseracing, developing an interest and expertise in the National Hunt that is widely regarded as second to none. By no stretch of the imagination can she be called the most successful of owners, but few can have been more permanently or deeply fascinated by the sport's vagaries, or less discouraged by its disappointments. Who else might see her one and only good Grand National prospect collapse inexplicably on the very point of victory, then shrug her shoulders and say, "That's racing".

Meanwhile, the Queen Mother ran her own very personal style of public duty, with a busy and wide-ranging diary of engagements at home and a genteel and colourful series of visits within the

Commonwealth. East and southern Africa, to parts of which she had travelled with the Duke of York only two years after their marriage, became great favourites, while journeys to Australia, New Zealand and Canada were frequent and picturesque. In between whiles, she paid visits to France, Italy and the United States where she became renowned for her smiling informality and ability to make new friends easily. Back in Britain, she belied her advancing years by retaining her Chancellorship of the University of London for twenty-five years until her eightieth birthday, and still proved the best dancer at successive Student Union Balls. And on a gentler theme, she pursued her lifelong love of flowers and gardens - born in childhood and nurtured from the earliest years of her marriage - by her active and continual patronage of the London Gardens Scheme. She shows a fascination for the arts, and especially music, that defies those who would called the royals philistines, yet will pitch into a few strokes of snooker, sway to Caribbean street-music, and pass the time of day with leather-jacketed rockers as naturally as if she had understudied for the part. She is aware that such opportunities arise out of her presence, and she is anxious not to spoil the show. Ask any news photographer who his favourite royal is, and her name will be your answer, because she responds to the opportunities they present to her, just as they have to respond to the opportunities she affords them.

Her family have always had first claim on her. While her elder daughter the Queen was away on lengthy tours abroad in the 1950s, it was the Queen Mother who looked after Prince Charles and Princess Anne. When the younger daughter Princess Margaret was on the verge of motherhood, it was to Clarence House that she came for her confinement. It was the Queen Mother who introduced Princess Anne to the world of competitive horsemanship, who painstakingly brought Prince Charles up to appreciate good music, who specially commissioned a bust to be made of her three-year-old grandson Prince Andrew, and who took Prince Edward and the children of Princess Margaret with her on her royal progress through Kent during the ceremonies marking her appointment as Lord Warden of the Cinque Ports. It was into her care that the young Lady Diana Spencer was put after her engagement to the Prince of Wales, and at Clarence House that she learned the royal skills that the Queen Mother had acquired almost sixty years before. And it was from Clarence House that both Lady Diana, and later Sarah Ferguson, left to marry their royal husbands.

She is, by certain standards, a remarkable woman, though she has justified the epithet by being a relatively unremarkable soul who has tackled, coped with and succeeded in mastering a series of remarkable circumstances. Her life story reflects, and has at times been moulded by, many of the events of this hectic century, some of which she experienced at uncomfortably close quarters. Whether, offered the choice again, she would opt for it is questionable, yet there is no doubt that, rarely tainted by controversy, refreshingly free of scandal, her story stands highlighted by years of contentment, colour, serenity and fulfilment. If it is tempting to begin it with the phrase "Once upon a time...", it is irresistible to end it with the words "...happily ever after."

Opposite page: Lady Elizabeth Bowes Lyon, newly engaged, in 1923. A signed portrait from the Royal Photographic Collection at Windsor. Reproduced by gracious permission of Her Majesty the Queen.

"My own happy childhood", as the Queen Mother describes it, was not especially indulgent for the era or the class into which she was born. But to us in a more egalitarian age, and in her own memory, her early years were uncommonly serene, carefree, quietly privileged, golden, quintessentially Edwardian. Early photographs **opposite page, top right** show her as a two-year-old, well worthy, in looks, dress and demeanour, of her aristocratic heritage. Her childhood moved between the family's Hertfordshire mansion, its London house in St James's, and the ancestral home at Glamis, where the pictures **opposite page, top left and bottom** were taken when she was about six. Occasionally she would be taken to stay with family friends abroad, and it was during a visit to Italy in 1907 that this beautiful portrait **above** was taken at the Stender photographic studio in Milan.

Previous pages: the Strathmore family at Glamis in 1904. Elizabeth's father, who had become the 14th Earl that February, stands between his elder children Fergus, John, Mary, Patrick and Alexander. Seated are Rose and Michael. Elizabeth leans against a chair in which her mother holds two-year-old David. David and Elizabeth's close companionship **opposite page, top** survived several arguments over ownership of the wheelbarrow **opposite page, bottom left** at St Paul's. **Opposite page, bottom right:** Elizabeth at St Paul's at the age of two, learning even then how to pose for the photographers. **Above:** a mature and beautifully-complexioned seven-year-old, showing an early preference for pearls and flowers.

Though the Queen Mother's interest in horses is deep and well-known, there exist few photographs showing her riding. One exception is this picture **below** of her sitting on Bobs, a mischievous but favourite pony stabled at St Paul's. A less animated pony was trundled around at Glamis **left** as her constant companion, until brother David reached an age at which they could share the pleasures of a carefree childhood. The photograph **bottom**, taken in 1911 at Glamis, was later used as a part blueprint for a painting of the whole Strathmore family, a copy of which now hangs at St Paul's Walden. **Opposite page:** Elizabeth and David at Glamis in 1913; by then, David had become a boarder at Eton, and Elizabeth missed him dreadfully.

22

The royal world into which Elizabeth's future husband was born lacked the pleasures normally associated with privileged Victorian family life. Born the second son of parents whose concept of duty and service pre-empted any feelings of affection for children, Prince Albert struggled through his early years at Queen Victoria's court. His look of slight bewilderment, betrayed in the photograph **top left** taken in the year of her Diamond Jubilee, never really left him – as the pictures, **top right** in 1905, and **above left** in 1906, show. Meanwhile, the young Lady Elizabeth blossomed under the influence of a benign, intelligent mother who saw no inconsistency in combining in her children a sense of responsibility and a search for enjoyment. The jester's uniform in which brother David dressed to partner a very Elizabethan Elizabeth for these pictures **above right and opposite page**, taken in 1909, can still be seen at Glamis today, as can the old chest from which all their dressing-up clothes were eagerly pulled.

Opposite page: Prince Albert's predictable and regimented royal upbringing took him eventually into the Navy. It became his greatest love, and a host of photographs showing him in naval uniform include that taken in 1917 **top left**, just before he joined his last ship HMS *Malaya*. He transferred to the Royal Naval Air Service **top right** on 1st

January 1918. In 1920, when the photograph **bottom left** was taken, his father King George V created him Duke of York, and the lady he became engaged to on January 14th, 1923 **bottom right** became Duchess of York on their marriage the following April. **Above:** this early portrait of the married couple comes from the Royal Collection at Windsor.

Right: Lady Elizabeth at twenty. By now she had made her debut in Society, and been presented at Court. David, up-and-coming at eighteen, was about to leave Eton for Magdalen College, Oxford when this picture **below** was taken. Until his early death in 1961, brother and sister remained close as Elizabeth continually visited him and his family at St Paul's. **Bottom:** Elizabeth, then Duchess of York, with David and his daughters, playing on a makeshift swing at the Hertforshire home in 1935. Three generations **opposite page** smile for the camera at St Paul's in 1931: David stands between Elizabeth and their mother, while the future Queen Elizabeth II looks pleased with the progress of small-scale building operations.

With the announcement of her engagement on 14th January, 1923, Elizabeth became a national celebrity. Portraits such as this one **opposite page** would soon adorn every shop window; and pictures of her with her mother at Glamis **above**, or receiving a wedding gift from her local Guide group in Angus **left** filled the illustrated newspapers. In mid-March, she and Bertie went **top** to the Edinburgh factory of McVitie & Price, where her wedding cake was being made.

When the wedding day came, all London was a festival. Crowds surged into the normally placid precincts of Bruton Street to see the bride **above left** leave her parents' town house for the Abbey, and to catch the first glimpse of the now famous draped, medieval-styled, ivory-coloured wedding gown threaded with silver, pearls and ribbon, and the train – modest by modern standards – of tulle, lame and Nottingham lace. This first marriage of a royal prince in Westminster Abbey for 540 years went beautifully, smooth as an everyday event, punctuated by rousing hymns and a sonorous yet touching address by the Archbishop of York. Afterwards, the official photographs recorded the event, if rather solemnly **above**, and brought into prominence Elizabeth's closest personal friends **top** whom she had chosen as bridesmaids. **Opposite page:** The new Duchess of York shortly after her marriage. **Left:** an official portrait of the Duke and Duchess taken to mark their tour of Australasia in 1927.

With Elizabeth's marriage into the Royal Family came introductions to a new circle of loyal and discreet family friends. King George V's Private Secretary, Lord Stamfordham, played host to the King and Queen and the Duke and Duchess of York **top** at Broomhall in July 1923, while the Earl and Countess of Leicester, who lived at Holkham Hall, just a few miles from Sandringham, posed with Queen Mary and her new daughter-in-law **opposite page, bottom** during the Norwich Music Festival in October 1924. To Queen Mary personally, Elizabeth was a dependable companion, and no Balmoral holiday was complete without the Yorks. **Above:** this group at Balmoral in 1923 includes Prince George, the future Duke of Kent, who was killed while flying over Scotland during the Second World War. **Opposite page, top:** Queen Mary with "Bertie & E", as she often referred to them in her diaries and letters, walking in the walled garden at Balmoral in 1924.

Of the Strathmores it can truly be said that they did not lose a daughter, but gained a son. At least one annual visit by the Yorks to Glamis became *de rigueur* from the very year of their marriage. They spent part of their honeymoon there (though Elizabeth caught whooping cough – "so unromantic", the bridegroom noted!), and in later years their children were to remember blissful summer holidays at the old castle. The comings and goings of the Duke and Duchess on these regular excursions were nothing

if not unceremonial. Their arrival at Glamis station **opposite page:** in the summer of1925 is a study in informality, with the stack of assorted suitcases, grips and parcels unloaded at the foot of the passenger bridge, and the Duke looking for all the world as if impatient of the portering services. Meanwhile, the Duchess looks on – a picture of serenity – with a canine companion that clearly preceded the royal penchant for corgis. **Above:** a more formal study of the Duchess, taken in 1926.

Princess Elizabeth Alexandra Mary, born on 21st April, 1926, was named after her mother, her great-grandmother (Queen Alexandra, who had died five months earlier), and her grandmother Queen Mary. Typically of the modest profile which the Yorks kept on their private life, they chose as the baby's birthplace, not one of the royal palaces, but the Strathmores' Bruton Street house from which the Duchess had gone to be married three years before. The house has long since been converted for commercial use, but a plaque records the event which circumstances then unforeseen have made historic. The birth was neither easy nor convenient: the Duchess had to undergo a Caesarean operation, and the Duke had to awaken his parents at 3 a.m. to inform them of the happy event. "We always wanted a child to make our happiness complete," he wrote later, with all the bemused gratification of the first-time father, "and now that it has happened, it seems so wonderful and strange. I am so proud of Elizabeth after all she has gone through in the last few days... " A profusion of photographs followed, including **above** the pre-christening study of mother and child, and the portrait **opposite page**, taken that December – a happy yet poignant picture, since the Yorks were about to leave for a long tour of Australasia.

Elizabeth 1926

The christening of Princess Elizabeth, the King's first granddaughter, took place in the private chapel at Buckingham Palace – destroyed during the 1940 bombing, now the site of the Queen's Gallery. The photograph **above** was taken on the day, 29th May 1926, the baby wearing the Honiton lace robe in which royal babies have traditionally been baptised since Queen Victoria's eldest daughter in 1840. Of the six godparents, only Queen Mary noted for posterity that, "of course, poor baby cried." Indeed she revelled in her grandmotherly role as she never had as a mother. Though the Duchess of York came back from engagements loaded with presents for her new baby – she received this teddy bear **opposite page,**

top left at Ilford that October – Queen Mary had the lion's share of the child once the Yorks went abroad the following January. On the baby's first birthday, she asked Marcus Adams to take the photograph **opposite page, top right**, and it is widely thought that our present Queen's sense of duty stems from her affectionate respect for this most rigidly dutiful of Queen Consorts. But even Queen Mary had to hand the baby back to its mother when the Yorks finally came home – and of course there was another photograph **right**, complete with all four grandparents, to celebrate.

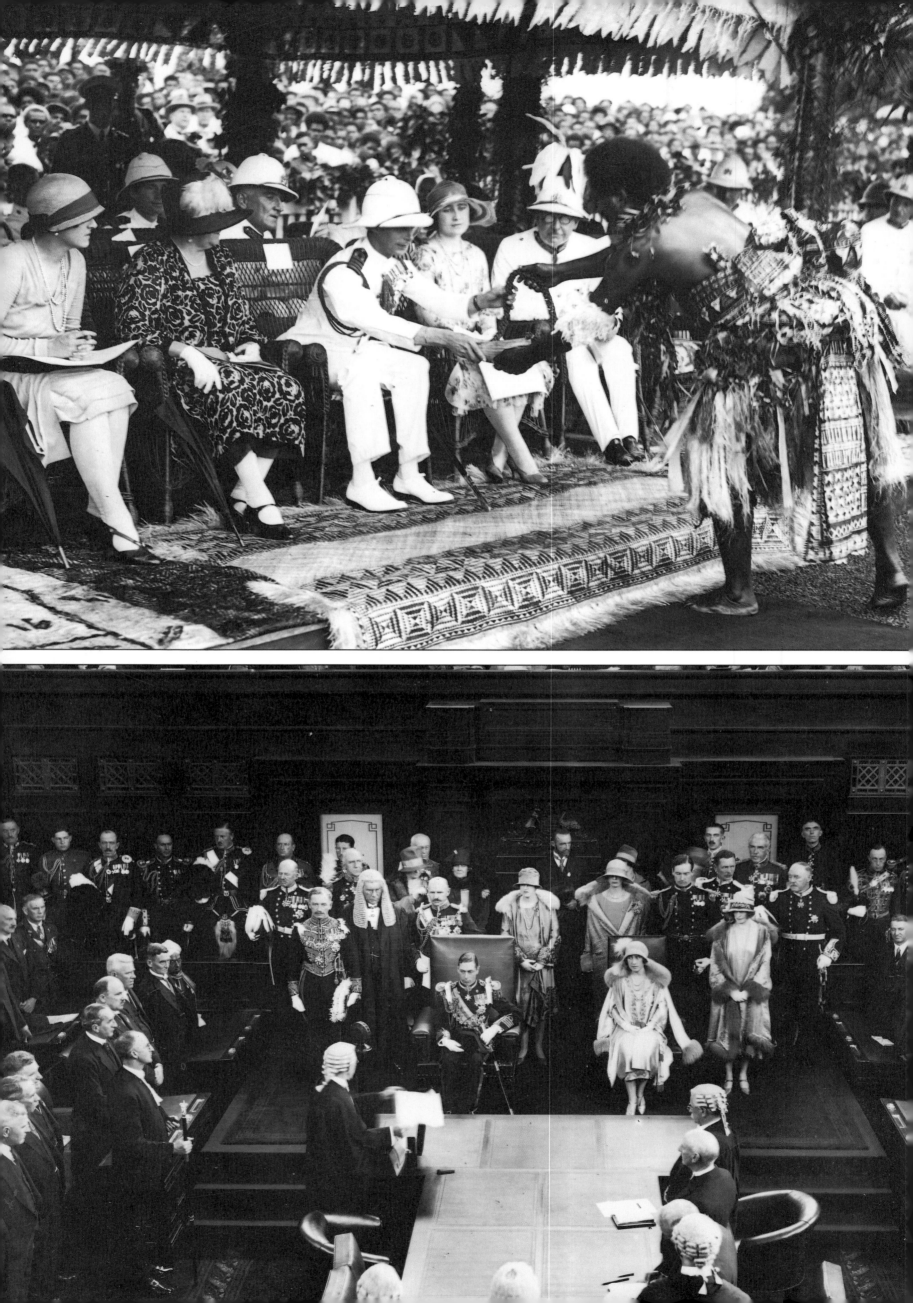

Elizabeth's first taste of prolonged and distant foreign travel came with the royal tour of East Africa in 1924-5, but her visit with Bertie to Australasia in 1927 surpassed all in variety, enthusiasm and historical significance. At Fiji **opposite page top** they received the tabua, or whale's tooth, as the traditional symbol of homage, and at another ritual welcome at Rotorua, New Zealand, in February **above left**, they were given Maori cloaks to wear. They met Australian Aborigines **above centre right** at Beaudesert in April, and the octogenarian Mr Hendricksen **top right** who, 64 years earlier, had formed part of a guard of honour for Princess Alexandra when she left Denmark to marry the future Edward VII. Other welcoming ceremonies awaited the popular York couple in Maitland **top left** and at Brisbane **above right**, but the main purpose of the entire Australian visit was to open, on behalf of the King, the new Federal Parliament at Canberra **above centre left and opposite page, bottom.**

Opposite page: the famous picture of the Duchess of York with her catch at Lake Wanaka, on New Zealand's South Island. She has maintained a skill at fishing ever since. **This page:** the royal couple on board *Renown* **top right** on their crossing from New Zealand to Australia in April; in the centre of a White Rose formed by schoolchildren in Melbourne **left**; leaving Maitland, New South Wales **above**; and attending a Guide and Scout rally **top left** in Adelaide.

Left: though a far cry from Royal Ascot, Adelaide Cup Day provided the Duke and Duchess of York with an afternoon's welcome relaxation during the closing stages of their Empire tour. Back home, more routine duties awaited them: **above** attending the annual Costermongers' Ball at Finsbury in 1928, and **top** at an inspection of special constables at Hyde Park. Meanwhile, young Princess Elizabeth – Princess Betty, as one Australian familiarly called her in a letter to her parents – was growing apace, and Marcus Adams' superb photograph **opposite page**, taken in July 1928, became a winner throughout the Empire.

Above: another Marcus Adams study of the Duchess of York and Princess Elizabeth, taken in 1928. Adams' soft-focus technique, and later his rural studio settings, made his photographs of royal children so popular that he was still being commissioned by the present Queen as late as the mid-1950s. **Opposite page:** another visit to Glamis, with the Duke nursing a septic hand, in 1935. The corgi had become a firm favourite, and these regular visits to the Duchess' old home were beginning to embed themselves into the young memory of Princess Elizabeth. Before long, she would be writing lengthy letters of thanks to her grandmother, Lady Strathmore, and visitors to Glamis today can see a magnificent ten-page missive from her, following a particularly happy stay there in Coronation Year, 1937.

Opposite page: Family gatherings formal and informal. Summer holiday excursions from Balmoral were then, as now, frequent and regular, and this one **top** in September 1928 took King George V and his party through the forests to Loch Muick. The Duchess of York, who saw in the old King kindly and affectionate qualities that his own children rarely detected, looks on indulgently as Princess Elizabeth – "Lilibet" – is approached with mock enmity by her cousin Andrew Elphinstone. At Royal Ascot, in June 1925 **bottom**, the party included Prince Paul of Yugoslavia (between the Duke and Duchess of York), the Duke of Connaught (between the King and Queen) and on the right, Prince and Princess Arthur of Connaught. **This page:** the Duchess of York, later to develop marked tastes in painting that would eventually characterise her residences, accompanied Queen Mary on this visit in March 1928 to London's Victoria & Albert Museum to see an exhibition of pictures painted by civil servants.

Princess Margaret Rose was born on 21st August, 1930. The beginning of her often troubled life was heralded by a thunderstorm over her birthplace, Glamis, confusion over the Home Secretary's attendance at the birth, and a contretemps with the King over the baby's names. Amid it all, as Queen Mary recorded, "E. looking very well and the baby a darling."

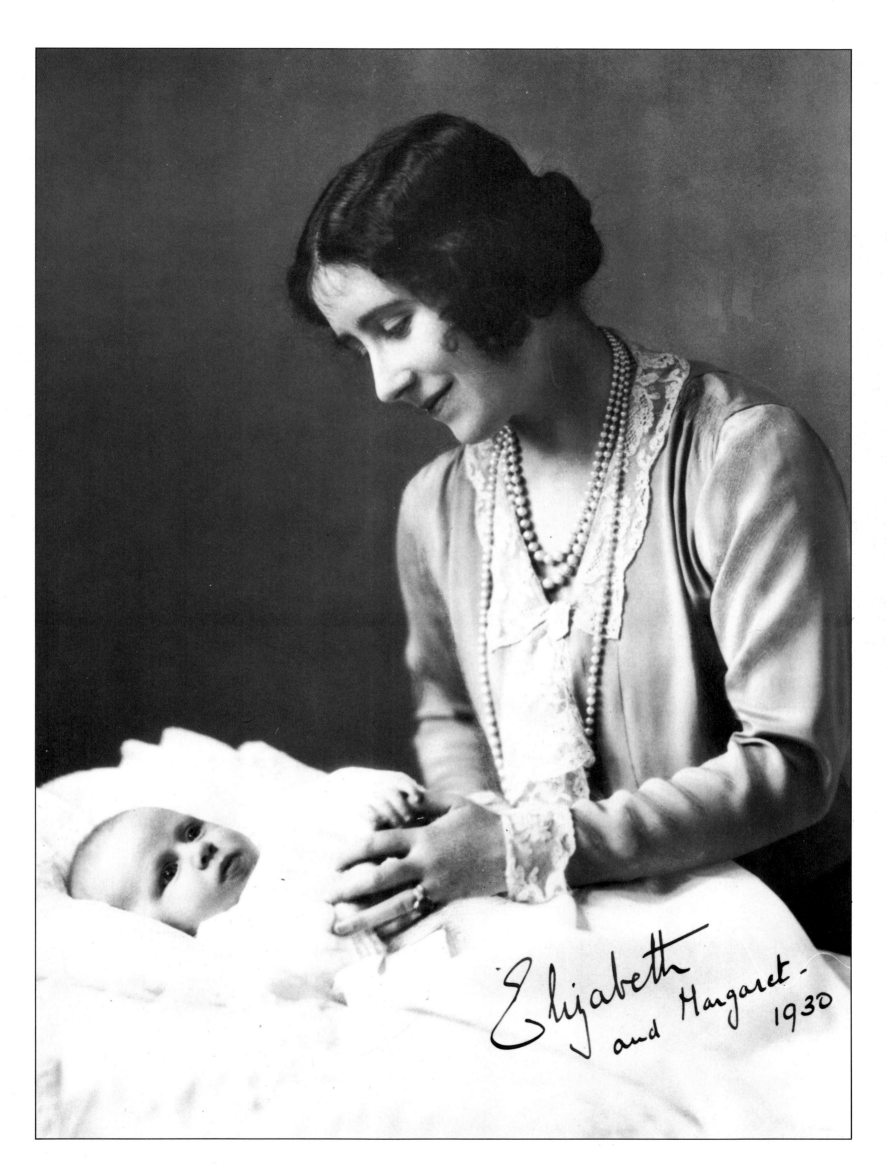

Elizabeth
and Margaret.
1930

Above: Princess Elizabeth in party dress, posing for this atmospheric portrait by Marcus Adams late in 1931. It was a big year for her: a new sister to look after, her first public outings, a grand family gathering at Glamis to celebrate the Golden Wedding of her maternal grandparents, and her first royal bridesmaid duties, at the wedding of Lady May Cambridge, daughter of Princess Alice of Athlone. It was also the year in which the Duke and Duchess of York took over Royal Lodge, Windsor, and in which the people of Wales presented Princess Elizabeth with the miniature cottage, *Y Bwthyn Bach*, with its delightful small-scale rooms and furnishings. The new little cottage was placed in the newly-landscaped grounds of the new big house where, in1932, the Yorks moved in. And the ailing King George, who had gifted Royal Lodge to them, came with Queen Mary to pay them a visit **opposite page** early in May the following year.

It has long been the custom with the Royal Family that a week or so each summer should be spent carrying out official engagements in Scotland. Clearly this was no imposition for the Duchess of York, whose roots even now continue to attract her north of the border several times a year. In July 1931 the Duke and Duchess of York accompanied the King and Queen to the Palace of Holyroodhouse, from which they visited the George Heriot Hospital **top** and Scottish National Academy **above**. The Scottish visit coincided with the great economic crisis which in Britain caused the downfall of the Labour Government, and the reduction of the King's Civil List by £50,000. The proportionate cut in the Duke of York's official income prompted him to give up hunting and sell his stable of six horses. He was not best pleased, and wrote to his equerry, "I am only doing this after careful consideration of the facts (damned hard facts)." The horses fetched £1,013.

Above: the Duke and Duchess of York with Princess Elizabeth and her cousin (later her bridesmaid) Margaret Elphinstone at a garden party for over 1,500 guests to celebrate the Strathmore Golden Wedding at Glamis during the second weekend in August 1931. Thirty-four members of the immediate family attended. The previous day the Duchess' parents threw a party and ball for the tenants of the estate. **Left:** the Yorks in November 1932, visiting the Imperial Institute in Kensington, where an exhibition was being held of goods made by disabled War veterans. **Top:** Lady of the Lamp; the Duchess, during a visit in June 1933 to Abercynon Colliery in Glamorganshire, inspects a miner's Davy lamp before he reports for the afternoon shift.

Above and right: Princesses Elizabeth and Margaret Rose at Windsor in 1933; both pony-riding and life at the little Welsh house had become great favourites. Their Scottish holiday that September included a visit to Abergeldie Fete **opposite page, top** and a private stay with the 86-year-old Marquess of Aberdeen at House of Cromar **opposite page, bottom.** The princesses' parents were back in Scotland for the annual Armistice service **this page, top** at St Giles' Cathedral, Edinburgh that November.

Opposite page, top: the Duke and Duchess of York visiting a
hospital in Cambridge in July 1932; and **bottom** making the first official
royal visit to the Isle of Skye for over 400 years, as they arrive at
Kyleakin as guests of Macleod of Macleod. More Scottish connections
this page, top as the Yorks attend the St Andrew's Eve Ball in
November 1935, and are welcomed to London's Grosvenor Hotel by the
Earl and Countess of Elgin and Kincardine. **Above:** three years after King
George V restored the public ceremonial of the Royal Maundy, the
Duchess of York and Princess Elizabeth, nosegays in hand, leave
Westminster Abbey after the service in April, 1935.

Life as both Duchess of York and Queen in the 1930s. **Opposite page, centre:** the Duke and Duchess of York join the King and Queen for the annual visit to the Isle of Wight in Cowes Week, 1933. With them are the officers of the Royal Yacht *Victoria and Albert*. **Above:** the Duchess with Princesses Elizabeth and Margaret Rose at the Royal Choral Society's 1934 Christmas Concert at the Royal Albert Hall. **Top right:** the Duchess of York with the Duchess of Devonshire at a Toc-H garden party at St James's Palace in July 1935. Toc-H's founder, the Revd "Tubby" Clayton walks behind them. **Top left:** an official portrait of the new Queen in 1937. She is wearing the Royal Victorian Order, and the personal Order of George V. **Opposite page, top:** the new Queen exchanges glances with Queen Mary, as the King watches the racing on Derby Day, 1937 – a surprisingly happy occasion, considering that the exiled Duke of Windsor was to marry the former Mrs Simpson the following day. Also in the Royal Box are the Duke and Duchess of Gloucester and Prince Arthur of Connaught. **Opposite page, bottom:** Queen Elizabeth with her two daughters, Queen Mary, the Princess Royal and the Earl of Harewood attending the presentation by King George VI of new Colours to the 2nd Battalion Grenadier Guards at Buckingham Palace in May 1938. **Opposite page, bottom:** the Queen with President Lebrun at a garden party in the Bois de Boulogne during the State Visit to France in July 1938.

With the Prince of Wales still unmarried, the York family became the focus of domestic public attention. The growing enthusiasm for monarchy in the Thirties led to an insatiable demand for royal photographs and the indefatigable Marcus Adams came to the Yorks' London home at 145 Piccadilly to photograph the Duchess with her two daughters **opposite page, top** in 1934. On the public duty front, Britain's economic recovery was slow, but morale was kept high by constant royal visits to factories, such as Firth & Brown's steelworks in Sheffield, which the Duchess visited **above and top** that July. **Above left:** with the Duke, after a visit to a disabled men's exhbition at the Imperial Institute, London the following November. **Right:** as Queen, with King George VI as Admiral of the Fleet during a visit to Portsmouth in Coronation Year.

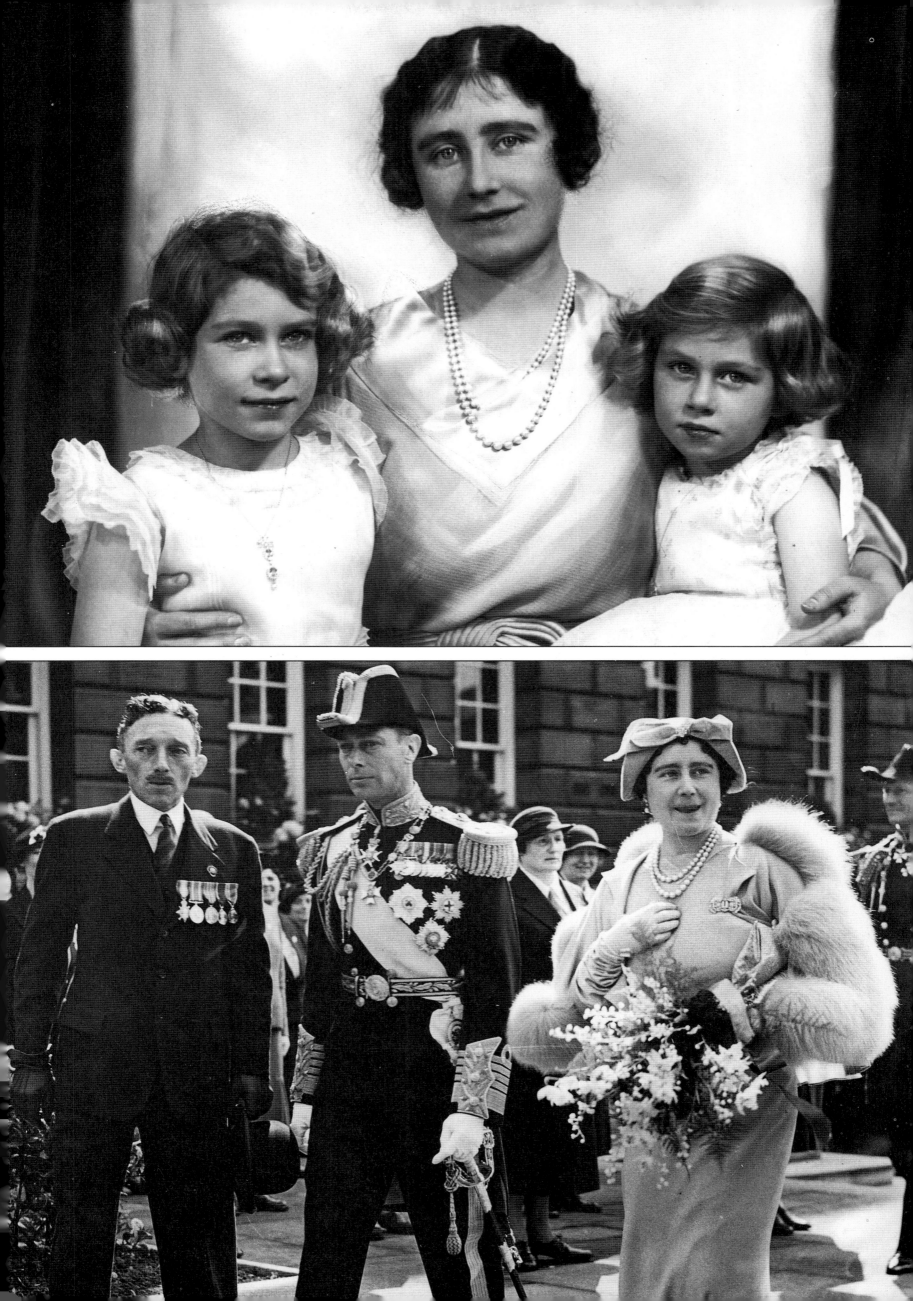

The highlight of 1935 was George V's Silver Jubilee in May. The entire Royal Family came to St Paul's Cathedral for the Thanksgiving service, including the world's most famous little princesses **left**, who accompanied their parents and the newly-wed Kents. The balcony scene afterwards **top** gave the public its best view of the family. Lilibet and Margaret wore the same matching pink outfits again that August, when their mother took them **opposite page** to see the presentation of Colours to the Black Watch at Glamis Castle. **Above:** the family at the Richmond Horse Show in Surrey, in June 1935.

George V's death in January made 1936 a busy year for the York family. In March the Duchess stayed at Compton Place, near Eastbourne after a five-week bout of 'flu, and with her family attended matins at Eastbourne Parish Church **opposite page** that weekend. There was great public interest in their appearance at the Royal Tournament at Olympia in May **top and left**, while one of many summer engagements took the Duchess **above** to the Heritage Craft School at Chailey, Sussex in June.

In April of Coronation Year, the new King and Queen took their daughters to a children's Coronation concert **opposite page, bottom** at London's Central Hall. In May, they reviewed the Fleet after a reception at Portsmouth's Guildhall **opposite page, top**. June saw the traditional royal visit to the Epsom Derby **left**, the first Trooping of the new reign, which the Queen, the princesses and Queen Mary attended **top**, and the first Garter ceremony **above**, when the Queen, recently introduced to the Order by the King, was formally installed.

"The curious thing is that we are not afraid," wrote Queen Elizabeth, shortly after her husband's accession. Nevertheless, the King confessed to a "sinking feeling inside" on the morning of his Coronation, when he left on a grey morning **opposite page, top** for what he described as "the most important ceremony in my life". By the time he got to Westminster Abbey, he had already been awake for eight hours, having been roused from sleep at 3 a.m. by the testing of loudspeakers in the Mall. "One of them," he mused, "might have been in our room". **Top:** the King is crowned, and Elizabeth awaits her own coronation as his Consort, before joining him **opposite page, bottom** for the service of Communion. **Above:** the King's procession and **left** the Queen's procession leaving the Abbey after the ceremony.

The massive crowds that assembled to see the King ride to his Coronation had begun to collect and lay territorial claims along the route as early as the afternoon of the previous day. Judging by the photographs, **above** showing the Coronation Coach turning from the Mall into Whitehall having passed through a beflagged Admiralty Arch, and **opposite page, top** at Hyde Park Corner, as the returning procession made for Marble Arch, even enthusiastic crowds with their seas of cardboard periscopes needed enviably little security control beyond the occasional mounted policeman. But the carnival atmosphere and demonstrations of loyalty and goodwill were no less than we marvel at today, and the King was impressed and thankful. In the days before the War, it was customary for the Coronation Coach to be used to take the Sovereign to the State Opening of Parliament. Accordingly, in October that year **opposite page, bottom**, Londoners were able to relive the pomp and circumstance of that memorable day in May.

The Coronation service, however, had not proceeded particularly smoothly. A chaplain fainted during the procession into the Abbey and delayed the King's arrival. The Dean of Westminster tried to persuade the King to put a robe on inside out. The King's bishops failed to indicate his Oath on the service sheet, and the Archbishop of Canterbury, coming to the rescue, held his thumbs over the words. The Lord Chamberlain fumbled so badly while placing the King's regalia on him that the King had to take over. The Archbishop probably put the Crown on the wrong way round, despite the King's best efforts to ensure otherwise, and arrangements for Abbey invitees were so bad that many were stranded there till 7 p.m., hours after the service ended. But from the Palace balcony it was all smiles as half a million people, unperturbed at having had three kings in a year, cheered their King and Queen to the echo.

Naturally, 1937, with all its continuing ceremony following the bleakest of years for the royal house, was a classic case of the *annus mirabilis*. The high ritual of the Coronation was followed by a veritable royal progress throughout the United Kingdom – London and the great cities of England; then a six-day visit to Scotland in July, characterised by this panoramic view **top** of the carriage procession driving along Princes Street in Edinburgh; then a shorter tour of Wales during which the medieval ramparts of Caernarfon Castle **opposite page** provided the setting for a monumental service of dedication not dissimilar from the investitures of 1911 and 1969; and finally a three-day visit to Northern Ireland. Never, perhaps, was the customary royal holiday at Balmoral more eagerly awaited, but even at the Braemar Games in mid-September, they couldn't resist bringing out the landaus yet again **above**.

Left: the new Queen greets her predecessor at the Armistice Day service in November 1937. Three days later, Elizabeth went back to her old home and with the King and her brother David attended St Paul's Walden Church **top** where she was baptised 37 years earlier. **Above:** the Queen leaving Harrods after ordering her Christmas presents, with just nine days to go! **Opposite page:** the King with the two princesses **top** riding in Windsor Great Park on Lilibet's 12th birthday; and **bottom** the King and Queen, with Lord Rosebery and the Princess Royal, at the 1938 Epsom Derby.

Opposite page, top: the Queen chats to Lord Elphinstone at Holyroodhouse in July, 1937 as the Royal Family meets the Company of Archers. **Above:** the King and Queen inspect new council flats at Shoreditch in March, 1938. **Opposite page, bottom:** the King visits an Air Force depot at Harwell, Berkshire in May, while two months later the Queen, Queen Mary and Lord Athlone attend a Girl Guides rally at Windsor Castle **right**, and the princesses come too. **Top:** Prime Minister and Mrs Chamberlain at Buckingham Palace that October.

Family, national and State occasions for Queen Elizabeth in 1938. In April **above** she attended, with the King and their children, the wedding of her niece Anne Bowes Lyon and Viscount Anson, who would become the parents of the present Earl of Lichfield. The marriage ended in divorce in 1948, and Anne later married Prince Georg of Denmark. One of the most brilliant of State Visits of the pre-War years took place in July 1938, when the King and Queen went to Paris. Elizabeth, dressed throughout as classically as at this garden party at the Bagatelle **opposite page, top,** enchanted the French. "Today," declared one newspaper, 'France is a monarchy again. We have taken her to our hearts: she rules over two nations." The visit was designed to confirm the Anglo-French *entente* in the face of rising Axis power, though it quickly became apparent that the outbreak of war was only a matter of time, and the Armistice service which the Royal Family attended that November **opposite page, bottom** was peacetime's last.

The 1938 visit to France was returned the next March, a week after Hitler annexed Czechoslovakia. The Queen looked relaxed enough on arrival **left** at the French Embassy in London for a dinner, before hosting President Lebrun at a Covent Garden ballet. But the mood seemed to have changed **top** during the playing of anthems at Covent Garden, as if there were time to reflect on the uneasy significance of the occasion. Left to right are the Earl of Athlone, Queen Mary, the Princess Royal, the French President, Lady Patricia Ramsay, the Queen, the King, Princess Marie-Louise and Mme Lebrun. **Remaining pictures:** a contrast in royal portraiture; the regal elegance of this official 1939 Cecil Beaton study **above** of the Queen at Buckingham Palace seems a world away from the photograph **opposite page** taken for private use in the same year. Though the latter is signed with a very royal flourish, it has found a modest place on a window desk in her sitting room at Glamis, remaining unpublished until now.

Elizabeth R
1939

These three studies of the Royal Family in the spring of 1939 were from a portfolio of official photographs taken at Buckingham Palace by Marcus Adams to mark the King and Queen's forthcoming tour of Canada and the United States.

King George and Queen Elizabeth arriving **top** at Ottawa's Parliament Building to preside over a session of the Canadian Parliament, and **above** pausing to greet their Canadian subjects before leaving. Their subsequent six-week tour of the Dominion took them from coast to coast. **Opposite page:** a moment of relaxation in the Rockies at their guest quarters at Jasper Park Lodge.

While in Ottawa, the Queen unveiled a War Memorial and then, at her own suggestion, decided to break with the schedule and go down to meet some of the veterans **top**. The Governor-General recorded afterwards: "It was an amazing sight, for we were simply swallowed up. The faces of the Scotland Yard detectives I shall never forget. It was wonderful to see the [veterans] weeping and crying, 'Ay, man, if Hitler could just see this.'"
Right: the Queen meeting Mayor Davison of Calgary and his wife.

Though shorter and snappier than the Canadian tour, the King and Queen's American visit – the first by a reigning British monarch – seemed replete with significance, and historic scores seemed finally settled with President Roosevelt's welcome **opposite page, bottom left** at Washington's Union Station. Their State drive in an open car **above** took them past the Capitol **left** on their way to the White House. **Top:** King George placing his wreath on the tomb of America's Unknown Soldier at Arlington Cemetery.

Contrasts in styles: the glitter and formality of much of the Canadian tour, as shown **left** as the King and Queen left Windsor, Ontario for Ottawa in May, gave way to a jauntier mood in Washington. **Opposite page, top:** the Queen stops to ask Girl Scout Leah Burket about her medal after a parade on the White House lawn; **opposite page, bottom:** President Roosevelt and his daughter-in-law take their royal guests for a drive round their Hyde Park estate. Contrasts, too, in the homecoming: the Queen clings to her hat as the King returns greetings **above** from boats in the Solent; while a more familiar welcome home **below** marks the formal end to a long absence.

The reunited family lost no time, in the short period before the outbreak of war, in making up for absence. July, at Dartmouth's Royal Naval College, was a family occasion with a difference, since there to greet them was not only Lord Louis Mountbatten **below** but also his nephew, Prince Philip of Greece **opposite page, top**. In August, the Queen and princesses **left** were with the King at Abergeldie for the last (in events) of his Boys' Camps, and all four **opposite page, bottom** joined in the famous Camp song *Under the Spreading Chestnut Tree*. **Bottom:** the Royal Family driving to Crathie Church that summer. The declaration of war broke their Balmoral holiday ten days later.

Top: On the very eve of war, the Queen, visiting ARP posts in London, goes into the Warwick Street dugout. "The phoney war" gave the King and Queen the chance to see those preparing for total conflict. **Left:** with officers during an inspection of Army training programmes in London, in late September. **Above:** the Queen visiting the Wrens' London HQ, January 1940. In April, she toured a salvage exhibition **top left** in Belgrave Square. **Opposite page:** in February **top** the royal couple, with Winston Churchill, met the crews of the *Ajax* and *Exeter*, and their relatives, for an investiture on Horse Guards Parade following the battle of the River Plate. By September, the war had come home: the King and Queen **below** survey German bomb damage to Buckingham Palace.

Opposite: the Royal Family at Windsor on the eve of Princess Elizabeth's 14th birthday. **Above:** "War has at all times called for the fortitude of women": the Queen makes her first wartime broadcast in November 1939. In the months before the German bombings, she travelled widely to see preparations for total war. In May 1940 **top**, she visited ARP personnel at an industrial plant in Lancashire, and in June joined soldiers from all parts of the Empire stationed at Victoria League Club premises in London **centre left**. Later, real bombs, real damage and real casualties sent both King and Queen out and about talking informally with the bereaved and the homeless, as **left** in South London in September.

Typical images of royal life in the Blitz-torn London of late summer and autumn, 1940. **Opposite page:** the King and Queen are taken on a lengthy tour **top** of some of East London's worst-hit areas, preceded by groups of curious children. Later, the Queen introduces a special walkabout **bottom**, meeting families who were daily exposed to the bombings. **This page:** the royal couple seeing at first hand **left** the extent of the damage and the good-humoured efforts to clear up, while **below** a visit to one of London's Underground stations cheers up a few children from families who saw their nightly trudge to these makeshift quarters as their only real hope of safety. The popular mood was not always favourable. There was a growing feeling, largely justified, that the poorer areas of London were suffering the worst of the German air raids, while the wealthier West End continued its privileged and largely uninterrupted life. At one stage, things got so bad that the King and Queen were actually booed and jeered in the streets of London, as popular morale continued to slide. In these circumstances, it was perhaps only to be expected that the Queen would welcome the bombing of Buckingham Palace as an event which did something to restore the veneer of common suffering, and this probably accounts for the immediate and lasting circulation of her most famous sentiment: "I'm glad we've been bombed; it makes me feel I can look the East End in the face."

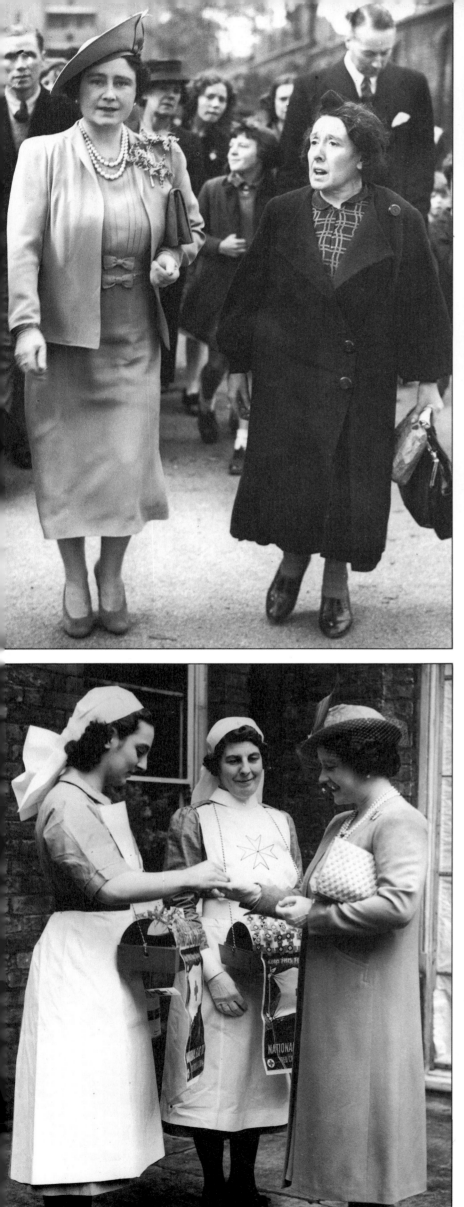

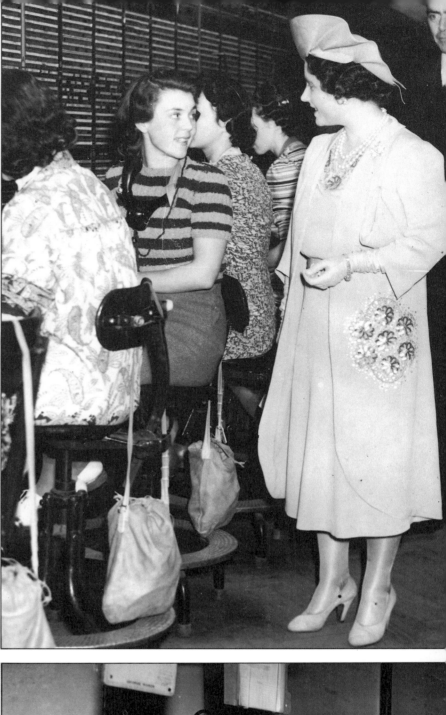

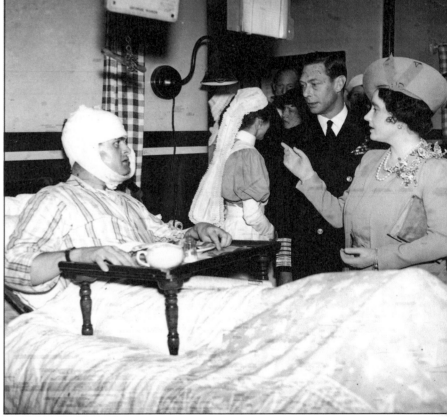

Two days before Buckingham Palace was bombed, the Queen was hearing from East End residents **top left** of their own air raid experiences. A fortnight later, she and the King visited a London hospital, itself partly bombed, and are seen **above** talking to a fireman injured on rescue duty.
Top right: the Queen visiting a London telephone exchange in 1940. There was no let-up in the war effort as 1941 came round. At St James's Palace for a meeting of the Red Cross, the Queen bought the first flag **left** for Red Cross Day. At Holloway Prison **opposite page, bottom** she received three rousing cheers from the prison's police force. Meanwhile, this picture **opposite page, top**, taken at Royal Lodge Windsor in April 1942, showing the Queen and her daughters knitting for the troops, was a typical example of morale-boosting royal photography.

Above: another classic Marcus Adams study of the young princesses, in the midst of tackling a huge jigsaw puzzle. The picture was taken in 1941 at Buckingham Palace, six months after they had made their first joint broadcast to the children of Britain. The King and Queen appreciated the importance of keeping their daughters very evidently at home at a time when many were convinced that, at the slightest danger, the Royal Family would be whisked off, like many European royals, to the safety of other countries. **Opposite page:** the King with his daughters, an alert corgi and a less alert Sealyham, at Windsor, ten days before Princess Elizabeth's 16th birthday. Though he inculcated his overwhelming devotion to duty in the elder daughter, the King found many of his lighter qualities reflected in Princess Margaret – instant charm, nimble wit, a sense of the ridiculous and a brilliant knack for mimicry.

Top: the Royal Family at Buckingham Palace, 1942. On her 16th birthday that year Princess Elizabeth became Colonel of the Grenadier Guards, Cecil Beaton took the photograph **left** of her wearing the regiment's badges and **above** she made her first inspection of the Guards at Buckingham Palace. Meanwhile, to strengthen the trans-Atlantic alliances, the King visited British aerodromes taken over by US Bomber Command **opposite page, top** while the Queen met Canadian soldiers stationed in Britain **opposite page, bottom**.

Top: the King meets crews of bombers that took part in raids over Essen and Cologne in June 1942. A year later, he was lunching *al fresco* with General Patton **above left** during a tour of US Army units, and in October 1944 was on French soil discussing liberation plans with General Eisenhower **above**. **Left:** the Queen joined the King on a visit to Bomber Command, where they watched 8,000lb bombs being fitted into aircraft, July 1944. **Opposite:** a pre-War portrait of Queen Elizabeth, taken by Cecil Beaton in the summer of 1939.

Above: a wartime record of a long and fruitful friendship. The King with Prime Minister Winston Churchill in the grounds of Buckingham Palace, shortly after His Majesty's return from visits to British and Allied armies in Italy. **Opposite page: top right** Princess Elizabeth joined the Auxiliary Territorial Service in 1943, undergoing the NCO's course in the theory and practice of mechanics, maintenance, servicing and driving at Aldershot. She was gazetted as Subaltern in March 1945 when the photograph **top left** was taken, showing her in the Motor Transport Section. Two months later, the end of war in Europe was heralded by endless celebrations, including the presentation by Parliament of Loyal Addresses to the King; the photograph **bottom** shows the King and Queen returning from Westminster afterwards. "We have been overwhelmed," the King wrote later, "by the kind things people have said over our part in the War. We have only tried to do our duty during these five and a half years."

Top: the Queen standing beside the King as he takes the Salute at the Victory anniversary celebrations in June 1946. He confessed that he found it "difficult to rejoice or relax as there is still so much hard work ahead to deal with." For Queen Elizabeth too, an official photograph of whom was taken that year **above,** the next few years were to be busy and at times traumatic, though there was little hint of it at the time. In October, the family attended the marriage at Romsey Abbey **opposite page, top** of Lord Louis Mountbatten's elder daughter Patricia to Lord Brabourne. The attentions of young Prince Philip of Greece (seen right of the picture) fuelled speculation that another royal wedding might not be too distant. **Opposite page, bottom:** the King, Queen and two very mature-looking princesses arriving for the first post-War Royal Variety Performance, at the London Palladium in November 1946.

Above: Queen Elizabeth in evening dress, photographed by Dorothy Wilding in 1946, shortly before the Royal Family left for South Africa in January 1947. The King felt guilty about leaving Britain at a time of severe austerity and horrendous winter privations, but growing dissatisfaction especially among Afrikaners in South Africa, left no doubt as to the necessity of the visit. **Opposite page, top:** the King, Queen and their daughters in the grounds of the Governor-General's residence on Grant's Hill, Bloemfontein, where they arrived early in March. Here, sweeping, stately processions through broad avenues and the polite welcomings of the Voortrekker descendants impressed both hosts and visitors alike. Later during their tour of the Orange Free State, they stopped at Ladybrand **opposite page, bottom:** where the Queen received a posy of local flowers from the daughter of a magistrate, guided deftly by the town's Mayoress.

Above: the royal visitors attending a garden party in Mitchell Park, Durban, escorted by Mayor Ellis Brown. In contrast to the formality of the royal arrival in Cape Town **opposite page, bottom left** the previous February at the beginning of the nine-week tour, there was a distinct air of relaxation when, just before sailing for England, the King and Queen went to the top of Cape Town's Table Mountain **top** with the South African Prime Minister General Smuts. Smuts welcomed the visit with a spirit of hope which was not, in events, fulfilled: "We do feel that

the grace and kindliness of the Royal Family have been a healing and reconciling influence on the differences which to some extent unhappily distract us in this country." **Opposite page, top:** a portrait of the King and Queen, from a 1947 photograph in the Royal Collection at Windsor. **Opposite page, bottom right:** the royal couple in July 1947, the day on which Princess Elizabeth's engagement to Lieut Philip Mountbatten was announced.

At Princess Elizabeth's wedding at Westminster Abbey that November the guests **opposite page, top** included royalties from all over Europe. **Opposite page, bottom:** the King and Queen's procession after the service. **Right:** the newly-weds emerge from the Abbey and **top** acknowledge cheers from the Palace balcony. **Above:** Karsh of Ottawa's classic study of the young couple.

Right: Queen Elizabeth arriving at Trinity College, Cambridge in June 1947, to celebrate the College's 400th year. **Top:** another college visit a fortnight later – this time with Princess Margaret and Princess Elizabeth at Eton. **Above:** the King and Queen leaving St George's Chapel, Windsor Castle after the fully-restored ritual surrounding the 600th anniversary of the founding of the Order of the Garter in April 1948. The King, who had reclaimed the sole personal right to make all future appointments to the Order, admitted to it both Princess Elizabeth and the new Duke of Edinburgh, and their formal installation was included on this gloriously ceremonial occasion.

Above: the Queen, watched by her husband and the Earl of Montrose, planting a sapling in the grounds of Brodick Castle during the royal visit to Arran in July 1947. **Right:** the King with Princess Elizabeth walking towards the Royal Box at Epsom for the 1948 Derby. **Top right:** Princess Margaret accompanying her sister and the Duke of Edinburgh at the London Casino in January 1949 to see a performance of *Humpty Dumpty*. **Top left:** Queen Elizabeth at a garden party in London, Summer 1949.

The periodic royal celebrations that punctuated the emergence of Britain from post-War austerity reached a climax at the festivities marking the King and Queen's Silver Wedding anniversary in April 1948. Announced by a new series of official photographs **above and previous pages** emphasising a quietly comfortable domestic contentment at Buckingham Palace, celebrations took the form of a Thanksgiving service at St Paul's Cathedral **opposite page, bottom right**, preceded and followed by glittering processional carriage drives in the Mall and the Strand **opposite page, bottom left and top**. Over 150 guests were given a three-course luncheon at the Palace afterwards, and in the evening a 21-mile drive through the streets of East and South London was followed by a joint broadcast. In it, the King praised the blessings of the happy married life without which he felt he could not have discharged his duties as King, while the Queen, as if mindful of those Cockneys who had that very evening cheered her, said: "My heart goes out to all those who are living in uncongenial surroundings and who are longing for the time when they will have a home of their own... The world today is longing to find the secret of community, and all married lives are in a sense communities in miniature."

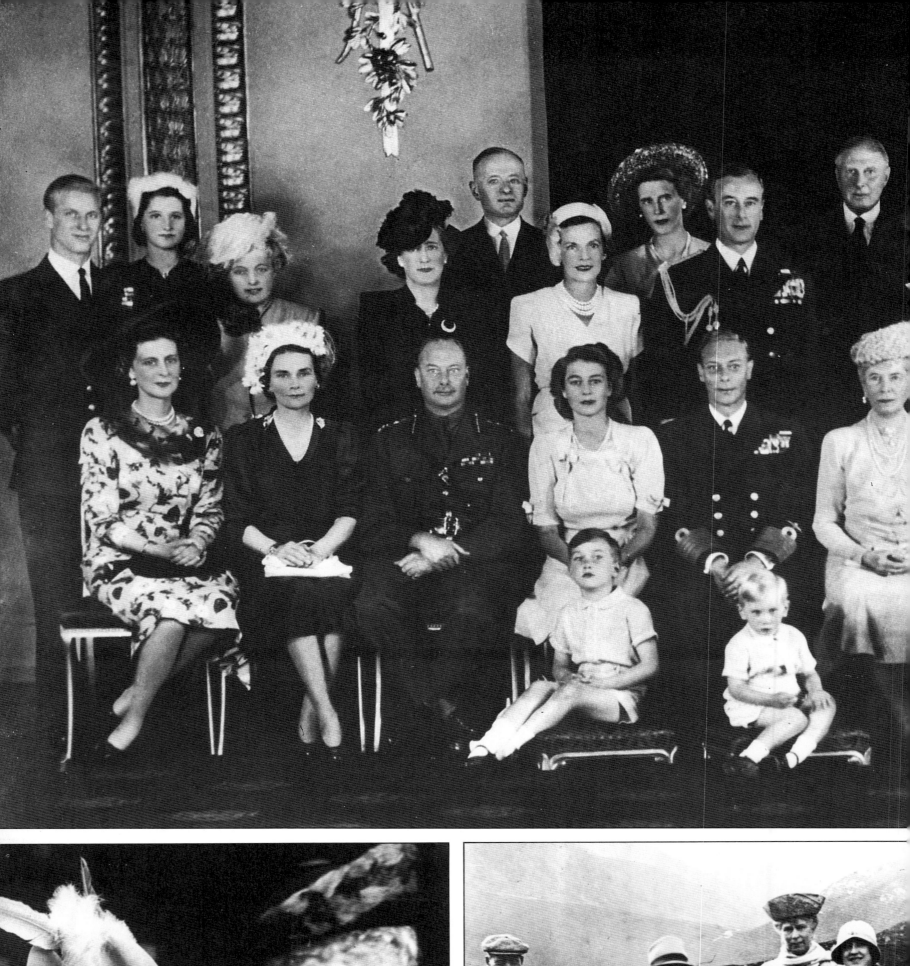

Queen Mary celebrated her eightieth birthday on 26th May 1947, when the photograph **above** of this large family group was taken. The juxtaposition of Queen Elizabeth and Queen Mary, sharers in their different ways of the same dedication to the concept of monarchy, was more than a mere formality. Their closeness is reflected in these photographs from Queen Mary's albums at Windsor. **Left:** George V, his cousin Princess Helena Victoria, Queen Mary and the Duchess of York at Glassalt in the Scottish Highlands in September 1927 – a snapshot taken by King Boris of Bulgaria. **Far left:** mother-in-law and daughter-in-law shopping in King's Lynn in January 1948. The following year, they attended a concert in King's Lynn **right** with a French visitor M Cortot, and Lady Fermoy, who was to become Queen Elizabeth's Lady in Waiting, and grandmother of the present Princess of Wales.

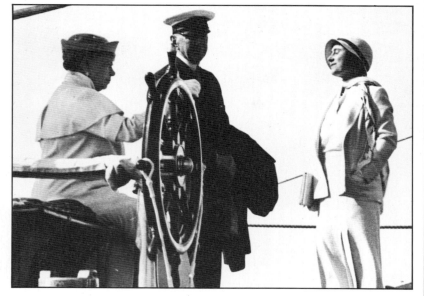

More from Queen Mary's photograph collection, including a trip on the royal yacht in the Solent in 1934 **above**, an affectionate greeting on Armistice Day 1937 **right**, a visit to the Welsh Guards at Warminster in 1942 **above centre**, and a family group at Buckingham Palace in 1946 **top** in which the guest of honour is Queen Wilhelmina of the Netherlands.

A portfolio of photographs from the Royal Collection at Windsor. **Top left:**
Queen Elizabeth with the widowed Duchess of Kent at Windsor in April 1944.
Top right: King George VI with his labrador at Sandringham, November 1949.
Above centre: the King and Queen with the Earl of Warwick at Warwick
Castle in April 1951. **Above:** the Queen Mother in her drawing room at
Clarence House, c.1956. **Left:** at the Catle of Mey in 1957.

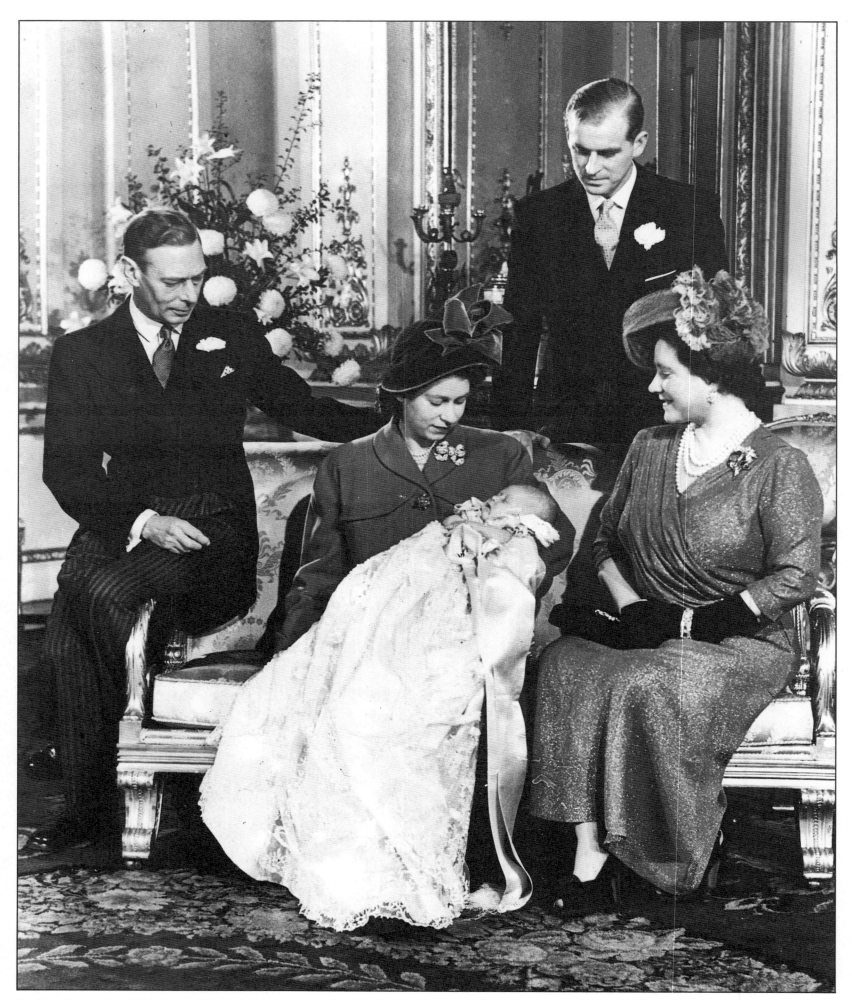

On 14th November, 1948 Queen Elizabeth became a grandmother for the first time, with the birth of Prince Charles at Buckingham Palace. He was christened there the following month, when this picture **above** was taken. There has been a chemistry between the prince and his grandmother from very early times. It was she who looked after him while his parents were abroad in his early years, who instilled his love of gardening, and who persevered in introducing him to the arts. "My grandmother," he once

wrote, "always made everything such fun, and expeditions exciting and enjoyable." In the following year, at a house-party after a day's racing at Royal Ascot **opposite page, bottom,** she developed her interest in steeple-chasing. **Opposite page, top:** the King and Queen, the Duke and Duchess of Edinburgh, Princess Margaret, the Duke and Duchess of Gloucester and the Marquess of Aberdeen at the 1949 Braemar Games.

Right: Queen Elizabeth watching the Oaks at Epsom, May 1950. **Bottom:** arriving at Royal Ascot with the King on Gold Cup Day that June. In July **opposite page, top** they attended the annual garden party at Buckingham Palace. In September, the Queen arrived at Dyce Airport **below** to resume her summer holiday after a trip to London. **Opposite page, bottom:** holding Prince Charles at his sister Princess Anne's baptism at Buckingham Palace in December.

Right: the Queen tours London gardens in Bethnal Green, July 1949.
Opposite page, bottom: launching the new *Ark Royal* at Birkenhead in May 1950. **Above:** with her brother David, visiting the Royal Horticultural Society's Orchid Show at Westminster in March 1951.
Top: with the King and Princess Margaret, passing ranks of King's Scholars at Westminster Abbey after the 1951 Maundy Service.
Opposite page, top: deputising for the King at a service of commemoration for 28,000 American servicemen killed while in action from British bases during the War: St Paul's Cathedral, July 1951.

1951, the last full year of the King's life, was a busy and worrying one for the Queen, whose self-possession was admired both at the time and in hindsight. In May the King opened the Festival of Britain, and led the Royal Family on a tour of the South Bank site **top**. Queen Mary followed, chatting constantly to her daughter-in-law, thrilled by the historical reflection that her own mother attended the 1851 exhibition at the age of 17, and here *she* was at the 1951 show at the ripe old age of almost 84. At the end of that month the Queen, without her husband, was at Epsom again, escorted by Lord Rosebery **opposite page**, and the following month she took Prince Charles **above** to watch Princess Elizabeth take the Salute at the King's birthday parade.

A twilight summer for King George VI in Scotland. On 3rd August, 1951 the Royal Family, with nurse Mabel Anderson holding Princess Anne, arrived **left and below** at Ballater Station *en route* for Balmoral, to be greeted by Lord Aberdeen, who also welcomed them to that year's Braemar Games **bottom**, held at the Princess Royal Park, Aberdeen. Also in the royal party is the young Prince Michael of Kent. Princess Margaret's 21st birthday that month was marked by the issue of these delightful yet poignant family photographs **opposite page**, taken in the grounds of Balmoral. **Overleaf:** one of Prince Charles' favourite photographs: with his sister and grandparents at Buckingham Palace on his third birthday.

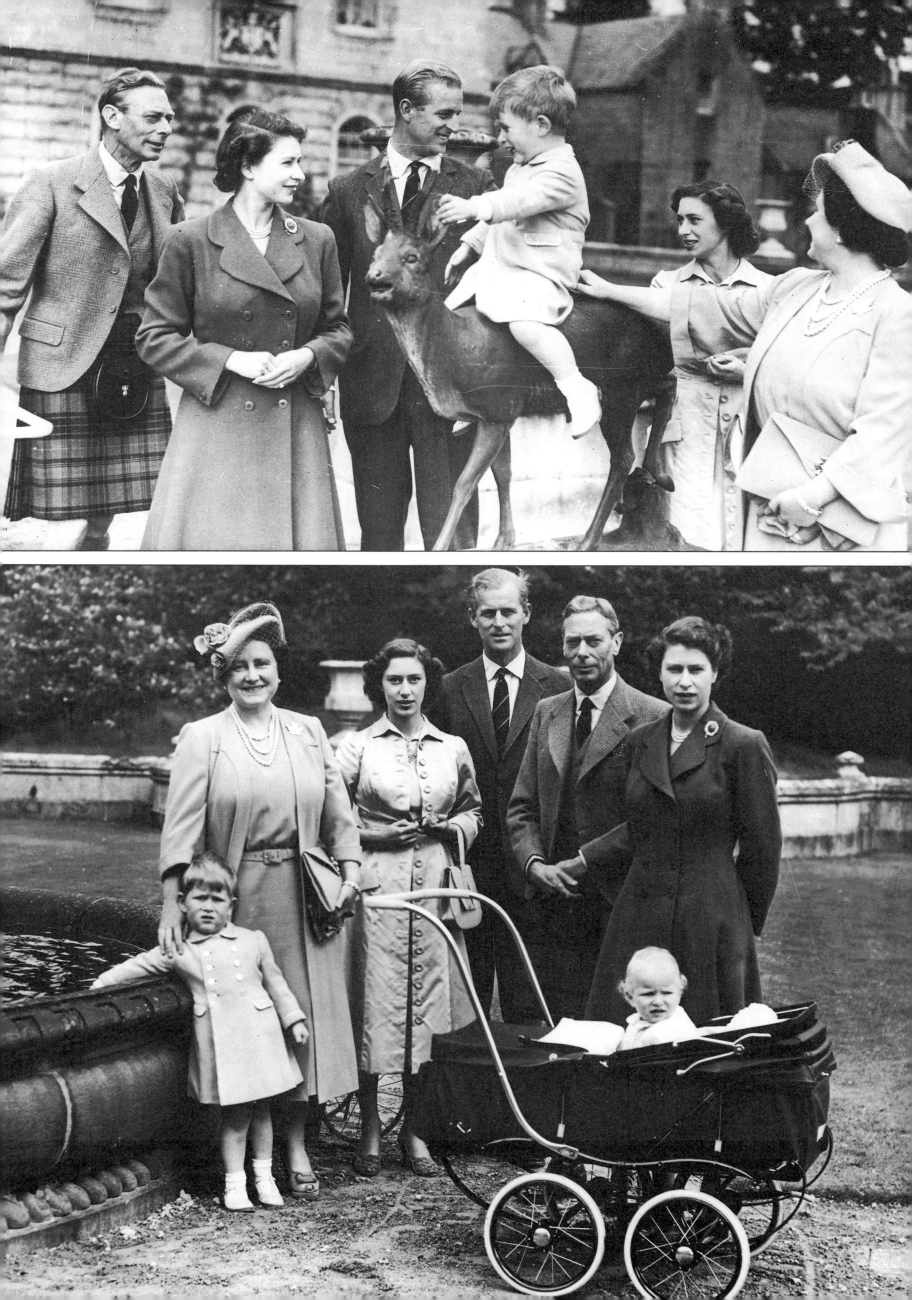

Previous pages: the King's last Christmas; surrounded by his family at Sandringham 1951. **Left:** the last official portrait, taken in November. **This page:** the last farewell; the King, with the Queen, Princess Margaret and Duke of Gloucester, see Princess Elizabeth and the Duke of Edinburgh off on a Commonwealth visit he was too ill to make himself, 30th January, 1952. **Right:** eight days later, the new Queen returns in mourning.

Top: Passers-by in London read of the King's death on 6th February.
Above: the widow, with her daughters, arrives at King's Cross Station,
London from Sandringham and is driven **top right** behind the King's cortege
to the lying-in-State at Westminster Hall . The procession **right** was simpler
than the subsequent funeral procession to Windsor **opposite page** which
took place four days later.

Previous pages: State dignity and personal sorrow. King George VI's coffin, covered by the Royal Standard and crowned by his widow's wreath and the message: "Darling Bertie, from his always loving Elizabeth", lies in State at Westminster Hall. The famous picture of the three Queens in deepest black states for all time the very essence of restrained royal grief. **These pages:** the King's funeral procession, having left Westminster, passes the Ritz in Piccadilly **above**, then Hyde Park **top** on its way to Paddington Station, where his coffin is borne into the waiting train **opposite page, bottom. Opposite page, top:** the funeral train leaving for Windsor. **Left:** Londoners observing a two-minutes' silence as the funeral begins at St George's Chapel, Windsor Castle.

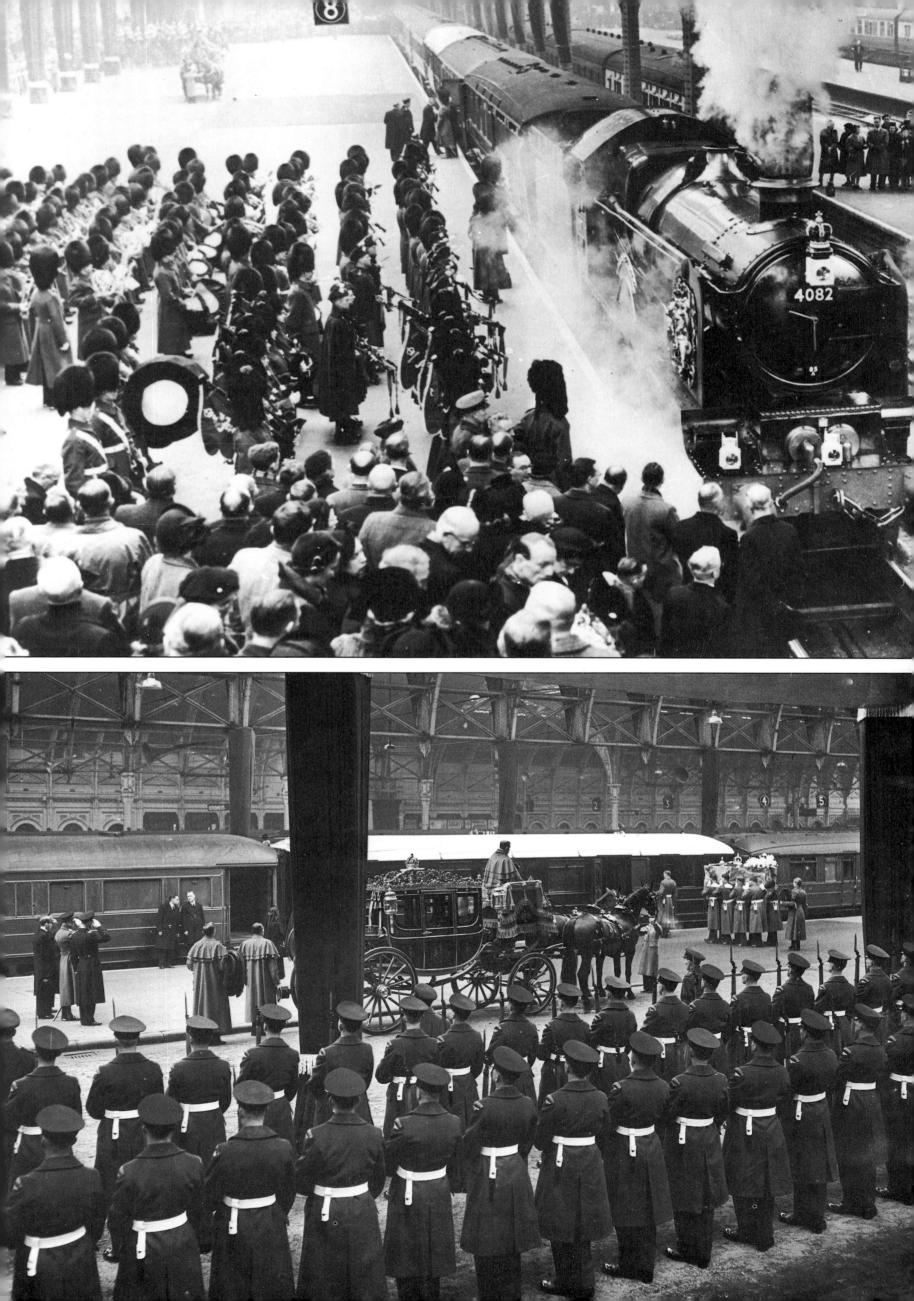

Queen Elizabeth was not slow in resuming life as a widow. Her first public engagement came in May, when, as Colonel-in-Chief, she inspected **right** the 1st Battalion of the Black Watch before they left for Korea. In July **bottom** she visited schools in Fulham. Coronation Year brought initial sadness with the death of Queen Mary in March – **below:** the Queen Mother driving to visit her on the day she died – but the pageantry and festivity of her daughter's Coronation **opposite page** were irresistible.

Opposite page, top: just over a week following the Coronation, the Queen Mother watched her daughter take the Salute at the birthday parade for the second time as Queen, and kept a weather eye over Prince Charles and Princess Anne on the Palace balcony. Two weeks later, attending a garden party at Lambeth Palace **opposite page, bottom left**, she received women from the Commonwealth. And four days after that she was on her way to the Commonwealth herself, leaving London **opposite**

page, bottom right with Princess Margaret for Southern Rhodesia. Back in Britain, she was again at the Braemar Games **top** in September: this time the young Princes Richard and William of Gloucester joined the royal party. **Above:** attending one of many National Hunt meetings at Sandown Park; arriving for the Grand Military Cup in March 1954 with Princess Margaret and the Duke and Duchess of Gloucester.

During the Queen's 1953-4 Commonwealth tour, the Queen Mother took charge of Charles and Anne. When the children went to meet their parents at Tobruk, she went to Balmoral for a short holiday, returning to London **left** to welcome the family home on 15th May. **Below:** Granny and Aunt 'Marget' take the youngsters ashore at Westminster Pier, after the Queen and Duke **bottom picture** disembark. **Opposite page, top:** home again! A happy fivesome on the Palace balcony. **Opposite page, bottom:** a family outing to Abergeldie Castle to attend a fete in aid of the Crathie Church Vestry Fund in August 1955.

In the Fifties the Queen Mother led a busy, varied life, fulfilling her promise at the time of her widowhood to do the work alone that she and the King had sought to do together. In November 1954 she went to Canada and New York, during which visit she attended a Columbia University Charter Day Dinner **top** at the Waldorf Astoria. **Left:** back home, meeting nursing staff at St James's Palace after attending a charity concert in December. In Scotland next August **opposite page, bottom** she unveiled a window at St John's Kirk, Perth, to Black Watch soldiers who died in World War II. **Opposite page, top:** attending a review by the Queen of Commonwealth VCs in Hyde Park, with other members of the Royal Family. **Top left:** visiting a school in Queen's Crescent, St Pancras in June 1957, as part of her tour of North London gardens. Three days later, she was off to Dunkirk with the Duke of Gloucester **above left** to unveil the memorial to 4,700 British Expeditionary Force soldiers. In July she was back in Southern Africa: **above;** she attends a Government House garden party in Lusaka.

Left: with Charles and Anne at the meet of the West Norfolk Hunt, January 1956. **Opposite page, top:** with jockey Dick Francis before the ill-fated 1956 Grand National. **Bottom:** a bevy of royal ladies at Ascot in June 1956, and again at Epsom **opposite page, bottom** on Oaks Day, 1958. **Below:** showing Princess Anne the Queen's plane as it arrives from the US in 1957.

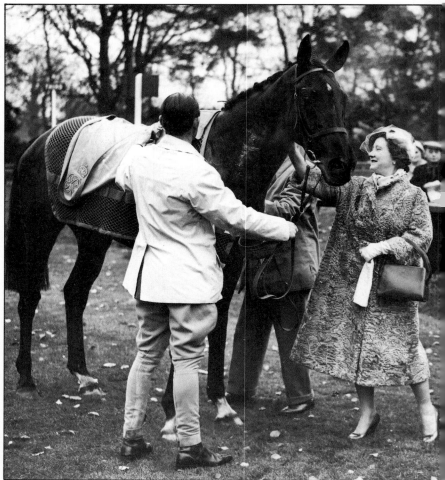

Top left: the Queen Mother arrives by helicopter onto the deck of the *Ark Royal* in Devonport in July 1958. **Top:** leaving St Clement Danes Church in the Strand after attending its rededication as an RAF Memorial Church that October. **Above:** a proud owner congratules horse and trainer after Double Star came 2nd at Sandown in November. **Left:** a week later, at the end of her third year as Chancellor of London University, she dances an eightsome reel with students at a Senate House dinner and ball.

166

In April 1959, the Queen Mother went for a three-week private and official visit to Italy, the country she used to visit frequently as a child and young woman. With her went her younger daughter Princess Margaret, still unmarried following her ill-starred liaison with Group Captain Peter Townsend, which ended in 1955. During the Italian visit, the Queen Mother and her daughter had an audience with the new Pope, John XXIII, after which this photograph of them leaving the Vatican **above** was taken.

That August, the Queen announced her third pregnancy, and was unable to attend the Braemar Games. Her mother deputised, and is seen **opposite page, bottom** meeting a young girl before the afternoon's events.
Opposite page, top: Princess Margaret became engaged in February 1960 to Antony Armstrong-Jones, and the future son-in-law joined the Queen Mother and Duke of Beaufort at that April's Badminton Horse Trials.

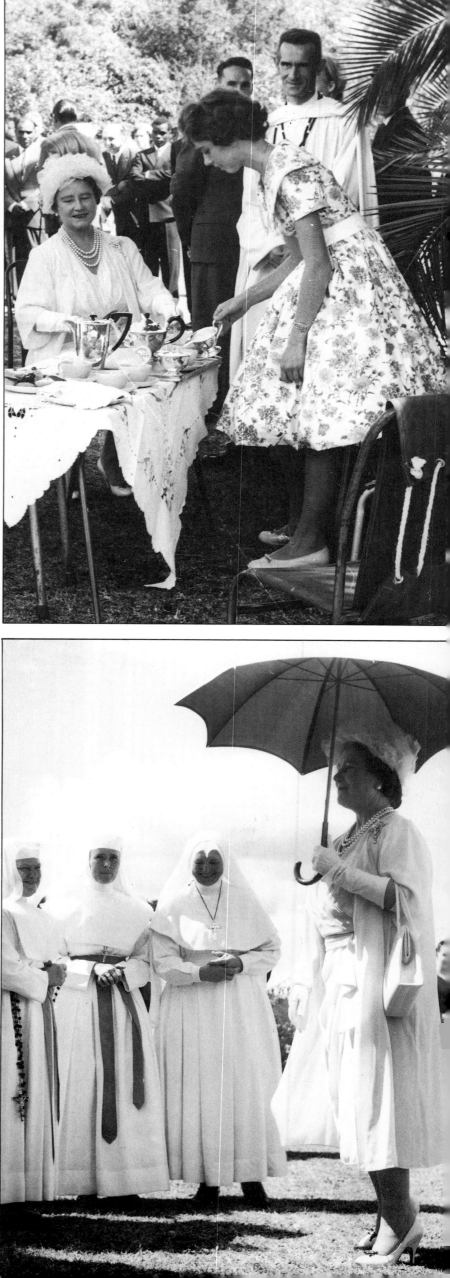

Opposite page: in Rhodesia and Nyasaland in May 1960, the Queen Mother visited Fort Jameson, where she attended a native council meeting and met chieftains **top left**, had tea at a garden party **top right**, and met the Grey sisters **bottom right**, all nuns from the same family at a local convent. She also attended the High Commissioner's garden party **bottom left** at Mlange, Nyasaland. **This page:** many happy returns; Charles and Anne bring 6-month-old Prince Andrew to Clarence House on Granny's 60th birthday.

The Queen Mother has been a regular guest of honour at the annual Royal Variety Performance, usually alternating duties with the Queen. Her turn came again in November 1961, when she brought with her to the Prince of Wales Theatre in London the newly married Duke and Duchess of Kent. Most Variety Performances have their unscheduled moments, and this was no exception. The French entertainer Maurice Chevalier, seen **opposite page, top** meeting Her Majesty after the show, finished his act with a rendering of the song *You Must Have Been a Beautiful Baby*, and dedicated it to her. **Opposite page, bottom:** the Queen Mother travelling from Clarence House to Buckingham Palace on 19th February 1963 to preside at an Investiture on behalf of the Queen, who was then on her second tour of Australia. With her travelled a birthday present for the three-year-old Prince Andrew, who twenty-three years later would bear the title Duke of York in succession to her late husband. **Above:** Anthony Buckley's splendid photographic portrait released in May of that year.

Opposite page: another Anthony Buckley portrait study of the Queen Mother. Taken in the drawing room of Clarence House in the spring of 1963, it shows her in a white organza gown with sprays of embroidered jasmine in grey and yellow silk thread. She is wearing her favourite diamond honeycomb tiara, a pearl and diamond necklace, diamond earrings and bracelet and her diamond fringe brooch. **This page:** contrasting fashions at the races. A warm coat for a cool spring Derby Day in 1963 **left**, as the Queen Mother studies form with the Duke of Ncrfolk; a light summery outfit **below** the following month for a carriage ride with the Queen up the Royal Ascot course; and **bottom** the warmest of woollen coats on a cold December afternoon at Sandown, where the royal cockles were no doubt warmed when the Queen Mother's Silver Dome came in with third prize. Early the following year, the Queen Mother contracted appendicitis, and went into King Edward VII Hospital for Officers for an operation. She came out again, bright and breezy, a fortnight later **bottom left**.

In 1966, the Queen Mother retraced some of the steps of her 1927 tour with her husband, when she re-visited New Zealand. As in Rotorua nearly forty years earlier, she had the customary royal meeting with Maoris **opposite page, bottom left**; there was a ready welcome from Sea Scouts as she arrived at Bluff, at the southernmost tip of South Island **opposite page, top left** on the wettest of days; and a visit to a stud farm was of course inevitable. On this occasion, the Queen Mother was guest at Inglewood Stud, near Canterbury, and met Afghanistan **opposite page, bottom right**, a horse she had seen race in Britain. **Remaining pictures:** another re-run of the 1927 tour as the Queen Mother tries her hand again at fishing – this time in Lake Waikato near Auckland. She caught a two-pound rainbow trout.

By the 1970s the Queen Mother had become generally regarded as the doyenne of an ever-expanding family. **Top:** leaving Sandringham Church on Prince Charles' arm, and surrounded by other family members, early in 1969. That November, she took Prince Edward and Lady Sarah Armstrong-Jones **right** with her to the Royal College of Music. **Above:** accompanying Mr Asger Henriksen, after the marriage of his daughter to the present Duke of Gloucester at Barnwell in 1972. **Opposite page:** with Prince Charles after his installation as a Knight of the Garter at Windsor in 1968.

6

Above: Queen Elizabeth the Queen Mother at 70 – one of several photographs taken by Cecil Beaton at Royal Lodge Windsor. This new milestone in the Queen Mother's long life was not celebrated officially, but with it began the unofficial custom of her annual public birthday appearances at Clarence House to receive flowers and presents from increasing crowds of well-wishers. **Opposite page, bottom:** the Queen Mother attending the Queen and Prince Philip's Silver Wedding service in Westminster Abbey in November 1972. **Opposite page, top:** a less formal, yet rather more tense, family occasion as the Queen Mother joins the Queen, Prince Philip, Princess Margaret, Viscount Linley and their host, the Duke of Beaufort, around the closed-circuit television at the Badminton Horse Trials in April 1973. Princess Anne and a young lieutenant named Mark Phillips were taking part in the competition.

Above: with Prince Charles at Clarence House in 1975: this photograph, taken by Peter Sellers, was issued to mark the Queen Mother's 75th birthday, and is now in the Princess of Wales' sitting room at Kensington Palace. **Left:** the Queen Mother with Earl Mountbatten at Holyroodhouse during King Carl XVI of Sweden's State Visit in 1975. **Top:** the Royal Family leaving church at Sandringham on the 25th anniversary of the death of George VI. **Opposite:** favourite grandsons; with Prince Charles at Ascot **top** in 1978, and greeted by trainee pilot Prince Andrew at RAF Leeming **bottom** in 1980.

Opposite page: Princess Anne provided the Queen Mother's first great-grandchild, Peter Phillips, in November 1977. Just before Christmas he was christened at Buckingham Palace and the traditional four generations photograph **top left** recorded the event. **Top right:** the Queen Mother with the Prince of Wales after a service at St Paul's Cathedral honouring ten great generals of World War II in November 1979. **Bottom left:** the Queen Mother enjoys the annual ceremony of distributing shamrocks to the Irish Guards – even if they do tend to be over a foot taller than she is! – and 1980 was no exception. **Bottom right:** the Queen Mother, in June 1980, with the Grand Duke of Luxemburg, who had just been installed as a Knight of the Garter at Windsor. **This page, top:** with 16-year-old Prince Edward on the way to the 1980 Trooping the Colour ceremony. **Above:** escorted by Prince Charles that July on her way to the Thanksgiving service at St Paul's Cathedral for her eightieth birthday.

The eightieth birthday celebrations took place three weeks before the actual anniversary, but it was no less happy an occasion for all that. St Paul's Cathedral fairly bristled with flowers, the Archbishop of Canterbury gave an address which seemed to reflect the mood of the whole nation, and the Queen, usually reserved on formal occasions, could hardly contain her delight **left**. Prince Charles escorted her out of the Cathedral to acknowledge the cheers of

the crowds outside **below**, before the familiar balcony appearance put her and her family on show **bottom** for all to see. When her birthday did come round on 4th August, the family was there again, this time to help with the enormous deliveries of bouquets, sweets and other gifts that were pressed into the Queen Mother's arms **this page**.

On 29th July, 1981 Prince Charles married Lady Diana
Spencer, and the Queen Mother witnessed the happy event.
Top: a short pause before going into St Paul's Cathedral
for the service. **Left:** the solemn moment of blessing for
bride and groom. **Opposite page, bottom left:**
driving back with Prince Andrew. **Opposite page, top:**
the bridal and family group assembled at Buckingham
Palace. **Above:** still going strong, the Queen Mother at
Lloyds of London in November 1981. **Opposite page,
bottom right:** the christening of Prince William in
1982; on her 82nd birthday, the Queen Mother cradles the
great-grandson who will one day become King.

Notable Events in the Life of the Queen Mother

1900 Seiges and reliefs of Ladysmith, Mafeking and Kimberley in the Boer War.
Boxer rebellion in China.
Lord Salisbury's Conservative government returned to power after a General Election.
Proclamation of the Australian Commonwealth.

1901 Trans-Siberian railway opened.
Death of Queen Victoria.
First transmission by Marconi across the Atlantic.
Assassination of President McKinley of the USA.

1902 Death of Cecil Rhodes.
Boer War ended by the Peace of Vereeniging.
Arthur Balfour becomes Prime Minister in succession to Lord Salisbury.
Coronation of King Edward VII and Queen Alexandra.

1903 Revelation of Belgian atrocities in the Congo.
The Wright brothers make their first powered flight.
Founding of the *Daily Mirror*.
Inauguration of the first manufactured Ford cars.

1904 Britain concludes treaty with Tibet.
Outbreak of war between Japan and Russia.
Conclusion of the Entente Cordiale between Britain and France.

1905 Abortive revolution in Russia following the events of "Bloody Sunday".
Opening of London's first electric Underground system.
Building commences of the first *Dreadnought* battleship.

1906 San Francisco destroyed by earthquake.
Conservatives defeated by the Liberals in the General Election.
First campaign by Suffragettes in London.
Discovery of vitamins.

1907 New Zealand becomes a Dominion.
Formation of the Triple Entente by Great Britain, France and Russia.
Baden-Powell founds the Boy Scout Movement.

1908 Belgium formally annexes the Congo.
Austria annexes Bosnia and Hertzegovina.
Asquith becomes Prime Minister of Britain.

1909 Old-age pensions first introduced..
First flight across the Channel made by Bleriot.
Two-year constitutional crisis prompted by the House of Lords' rejection of the Lloyd George budget.

Opposite page: the Queen Mother meets the Archbishop of Canterbury's special envoy, Terry Waite after she opened the London City YMCA at the Barbican Centre in April 1985.

1910 First Labour Exchange established.
Death of King Edward VII.
Doctor Crippen arrested on board ship *en route* to Canada.

1911 Britain introduces the National Insurance system.
Anarchists beseiged in Sidney Street in London.
King George V and Queen Mary attend the Imperial Durbar in Delhi.

1912 China becomes a republic.
Titanic sinks with the loss of over 1,500 lives.
Captain Scott reaches the South Pole.

1913 George V and Queen Mary visit the Kaiser at a family wedding in Germany.
Treaty of Bucharest ends a year of war and crisis in the Balkans.
Woodrow Wilson becomes President of the USA.

1914 Assassination of Archduke Franz Ferdinand of Austria.
Outbreak of World War I.
Britain proclaims a protectorate over Egypt.

1915 Sinking of the *Lusitania*.
First Zeppelin raid on London.
First Gallipoli landings.

1916 Britain adopts "Summer Time" daylight saving.
Evacuation of Gallipoli.
Death of Lord Kitchener.
Battle of the Somme.

1917 Balfour Declaration recognises Palestine as the Jewish national home.
Abdication of the Tsar of Russia in the wake of the First Russian Revolution.
America enters the First World War.
Lenin seizes power in Russia.

1918 Assassination of the Tsar of Russia and his family at Ekaterinburg.
Declaration of Armistice to end World War I.
Revolutionary movement begins in Germany.

1919 Lady Nancy Astor becomes the first woman MP.
Alcock and Brown make the first non-stop transatlantic flight.
Peace treaty signed at Versailles.

1920 Disintegration of the Ottoman Empire.
Introduction of Prohibition in America.
Cenotaph unveiled by King George V.

1921 Establishment of the Irish Free State.
First telephone kiosk introduced in Britain.
Greece declares war on Turkey.

1922 Death of Shackleton in the Falklands.
Mussolini seizes power in Italy.
Discovery of the tomb of Tutankhamen.

1923 Tokyo and Yokohama destroyed by earthquake.
Stanley Baldwin becomes Prime Minister.
FA Cup Final played for the first time at Wembley.

1924 Greek monarchy under George II overthrown.
Ramsay MacDonald becomes Britain's Prime Minister, heading the first Labour Government.
Death of Lenin.

1925 Hindenburg declared President of Germany.
Conclusion of the Locarno Treaties.
Summer Time made permanent in Britain.

1926 Establishment of the kingdom of Saudi-Arabia.
The first and only general strike takes place in Britain.
British forces make final evacuation of German territory.
Birth of Queen Elizabeth II.

1927 Canberra inaugurated as the new capital of the Australian Commonwealth.
Lindbergh makes a flight from New York to Paris in thirty-seven hours.

1928 Corinth destroyed in Greek earthquake.
Death of Earl Haig.
Universal suffrage takes effect in Britain.
First German passenger airship crosses the Atlantic.

1929 First engine-powered flight over the South Pole.
The Labour party comes to power in Britain.
The Wall Street Crash begins an international recession.

1930 Amy Johnson makes her solo flight from Britain to Australia.
R101 airship disaster at Beauvais, France.
Birth of Princess Margaret Rose.

1931 Spanish monarchy overthrown.
Britain claims Princess Elizabeth Land, Antarctica.
Britain abandons the Gold Standard.

1932 Sydney Harbour Bridge opened.
Inauguration of the Northern Ireland Parliament building, Stormont.
King George V makes the first royal Christmas broadcast.

1933 Hitler becomes Chancellor of Germany.
German Reichstag set on fire.
Roosevelt becomes President of the USA.

1934 Assassination of the Austrian Chancellor Dollfuss.
Queen Mary launches the liner *Queen Mary*, Clydebank.
Fred Perry wins Wimbledon for the first of three consecutive years.

1935 King George V's Silver Jubilee.
Mussolini invades Abyssinia.
National Government returned to power under Stanley Baldwin.

1936 Death of King George V at Sandringham.
Hitler invades the Rhineland.
First national TV broadcast in Britain.
Crystal Palace destroyed by fire.

1937 Airship *Hindenburg* disaster in New Jersey.
Neville Chamberlain becomes Prime Minister in succession to Stanley Baldwin.
Japan begins intended conquest of China.

1938 Opening of Singapore as a British naval base.
Annexation of Austria by Germany.
Munich agreement signed between Britain and Germany.

1939 Britain recognises the government of General Franco.
Invasion of Czechoslovakia by Hitler.
Outbreak of World War II following Germany's invasion of Poland.

1940 Winston Churchill becomes Prime Minister.
Much of northern Europe falls to the Germans.
Evacuation of Dunkirk.
Battle of Britain.

1941 America concludes the Lend-Lease pact with Britain.
German invasion of Russia.
Japanese naval air force attack on Pearl Harbour prompts America's entry into the war.

1942 Capitulation of Singapore to the Japanese.
Fall of Tobruk to the Allies.
German army halted at Stalingrad.

1943 Germany defeated by Russia.
Allied landing in Sicily.
Overthrow of Mussolini.
Teheran Conference between Roosevelt, Churchill and Stalin.

1944 Destruction of the monastery at Monte Cassino.
Allied entry into Rome.
D-Day landings in Normandy.

1945 Meeting of Churchill, Roosevelt and Stalin at Yalta.
Allied bombing raid on Dresden.
Allied celebrations of victory in Europe and, later, victory over Japan.
United Nations Charter signed at San Francisco.

1946 Italy becomes a republic.
War crimes trials begin at Nuremberg.
Churchill makes his "Iron Curtain" speech at Fulton, Missouri.
Trygve Lie elected as Secretary-General of the United Nations.

1947 Inauguration of Marshall Aid.
Princess Elizabeth comes of age and broadcasts her message of dedication to the Empire.
Lord Mountbatten assumes power as Viceroy of India.
The coal industry becomes nationalised in Britain.

1948 Nationalisation of railways and electricity in Britain.

The Berlin airlift begins.
Mahatma Gandhi assassinated.
State of Israel proclaimed by the Jews.

1949 Newfoundland becomes part of Canada.
Nationalisation of gas in Britain.
China becomes a people's republic under Mao Tse-tung.
Establishment of NATO.

1950 Russia and China sign a 30-year treaty.
North Korea invades South Korea.
Petrol rationing comes to an end in Britain.
New chamber of the House of Commons opened at Westminster.

1951 The King opens the Festival of Britain.
British oil companies nationalised by Iran.
Defection of Burgess and Maclean to Russia.
Winston Churchill becomes Prime Minister.

1952 BOAC inaugurates the first jet airline service with the Comet – London to Johannesburg in 23 hours.
Election of Dwight D. Eisenhower as American President.
Abdication of King Farouk of Egypt.
Britain tests her first atomic bomb.

1953 Conquest of Everest by John Hunt's British expedition.
Death of Stalin.
Mau Mau terrorism in Kenya.
Russia explodes her first H-bomb.

1954 Roger Bannister runs the mile in under four minutes.
Food rationing comes to an end in Britain.
French army defeated by the North Vietnamese at Dien Bien Phu.
Colonel Nasser assumes power in Egypt.

1955 Bulganin and Krushchev take power in Russia.
Retirement of Sir Winston Churchill as Prime Minister, in favour of Sir Anthony Eden.
Inauguration of ITV broadcasting.

1956 Britain and France invade Egypt and seize the Suez Canal.
Anti-Communist uprising put down in Hungary.
Marriage of Prince Rainier of Monaco to Grace Kelly.

1957 Race riots at Little Rock, Arkansas follow the enforcement of the Civil Rights Act.
The Russians launch the first Sputnik.
The Gold Coast becomes the first of Britain's African colonies to gain independence.
The Common Market is formed between France, West Germany, Holland, Belgium, Luxemburg and Italy.

1958 First major British race riots in Notting Hill, London.
Pope John XXIII succeeds Pope Pius XII.
General de Gaulle becomes President of France.
Fidel Castro overthrows the Batista regime in Cuba.

1959 Alaska and Hawaii become the 49th and 50th States of the USA.

Cyprus secures independence from Britain.
Formation of the European Free Trade Association.
The Dalai Lama flees from Tibet after China suppresses an uprising there.

1960 Harold Macmillan delivers his "wind of change" speech.
American U2 spy-plane shot down over Russia.
Sharpeville riots in South Africa.
John F. Kennedy elected as President of the USA.

1961 Yuri Gagarin becomes the first astronaut.
East Germany constructs the Berlin Wall.
Cuban exiles attempt the unsuccessful Bay of Pigs invasion.
South Africa becomes a republic and leaves the Commonwealth.

1962 United States' blockade of Cuba against the influx of Russian equipment for military bases there.
Algeria secures independence from France.
First American military advisers arrive in South Vietnam.
Adolf Eichmann executed by hanging in Israel.

1963 Britain refused entry into the Common Market.
Thousands killed in the Skopje earthquake, Yugoslavia.
Assassination of President Kennedy in Dallas.

1964 Labour, under Harold Wilson, regains power from the Tories.
BBC2 television inaugurated.
Formation of the Palestine Liberation Organisation.
Krushchev deposed as Soviet leader; Brezhnev and Kosygin succeed him.

1965 Death of Sir Winston Churchill.
Southern Rhodesia (now Zimbabwe) unilaterally declares independence from Britain.
First State Visit by the Queen to West Germany.

1966 England win the World Cup at Wembley.
Assassination of Prime Minister Verwoerd of South Africa.
Spain closes her frontier with Gibraltar.
Mao Tse-tung launches the cultural revolution in China.

1967 First heart transplant surgery carried out.
Six-day war between Egypt and Israel.
King Constantine flees Greece after right-wing generals stage a successful coup.
De Gaulle makes his "Vive le Québec libre" speech in Canada.

1968 Russian invasion of Czechoslovakia.
Richard Nixon wins the election for the US Presidency.
Anti-Government riots in Paris.
Assassination of Senator Robert Kennedy.

1969 Concorde makes its first non-commercial flight.
The USA lands the first men on the moon.
Death of Ho Chi Minh, President of North Vietnam.
Mrs Golda Meir becomes Prime Minister of Israel.

1970 End of two years of civil war in Biafra, Nigeria.
Salvador Allende elected as President of Chile.
Four students killed in anti-Vietnam War demonstrations at Kent State University.
Death of President Nasser of Egypt.

1971 Britain's currency goes decimal.
Death of Louis Armstrong.
Idi Amin assumes power in Uganda.
East Pakistan declares independence from Pakistan and is known as Bangladesh.

1972 Thirteen demonstrators shot dead in Londonderry on "Bloody Sunday".
Eleven athletes die in a Palestinian terrorist attack at the Olympic Games in Munich.
Governor George Wallace of Alabama severely paralysed after an assassination attempt.
Opening of the Watergate enquiry.

1973 Britain joins the Common Market.
President Allende overthrown in Chile.
Yom Kippur War between Arabs and Israelis.
Withdrawal of the USA from the Vietnamese War.

1974 Richard Nixon becomes the first President of the USA to resign from office in disgrace.
Emperor Haile Selassie overthrown in Ethiopia.
Cyprus partitioned following invasion by Turkey.
The Australian town of Darwin is destroyed by a cyclone.

1975 Margaret Thatcher becomes leader of the Conservative party.
Gough Whitlam dismissed as Australian Prime Minister by the Governor-General.
Restoration of the monarchy in Spain, on the death of General Franco.
Vietnam War comes to an end as North Vietnam overruns the South.

1976 Arrest of the Gang of Four in China, following the death of Mao Tse-tung.
Jimmy Carter becomes President of the USA in succession to Gerald Ford.
Concorde makes its first commercial flight.
176 killed in the Soweto riots in South Africa.

1977 Death of Elvis Presley.
President Bhutto of Pakistan ousted by General Zia.
582 killed as two aircraft collide at Tenerife airport.
Elizabeth II celebrates her Silver Jubilee.

1978 Israel and Egypt sign the Camp David Peace Agreement.
Death of Pope Paul VI and, 34 days later, of his successor Pope John Paul I.
Red Brigades assassinate Aldo Moro, the former Prime Minister of Italy.
The world's first "test-tube" baby is born.

1979 Conservatives win the General Election and Mrs Thatcher becomes Prime Minister.
The Shah of Persia is deposed and Ayatollah Khomeini takes power.
UDI comes to an end in Rhodesia.
Lord Mountbatten assassinated by the IRA.

1980 Death of Beatle John Lennon.
Mount St Helens erupts in America.
Ronald Reagan becomes the new President of the USA.
Russia invades Afghanistan.

1981 IRA prisoners' hunger strike campaign in Northern Ireland.
Columbia space shuttle successfully tested.
Assassination of President Sadat of Egypt.
Wedding of the Prince of Wales and Lady Diana Spencer.

1982 Britain liberates the Falkland Islands from Argentinian invasion.
Henry VIII's flagship *Mary Rose* raised over 500 years after sinking off Portsmouth.
Andropov succeeds Brezhnev as Soviet leader.
Over 200 killed in a Christian militia attack on a Palestinian refugee camp in Beirut.

1983 First issue of new £1 coins in Britain.
America invades Grenada.
Bob Hawke becomes Prime Minister of Australia as Labour regain power.
Conservatives win the British general election with a landslide majority.

1984 The IRA explode a bomb at the Brighton hotel housing the Prime Minister and members of the Government during the Conservative party conference.
Andropov of the USSR is succeeded by Konstantin Chernenko after only 15 months.
Mrs Gandhi is assassinated in the grounds of her Presidential palace.
Extensive famine in Ethiopia and the Sudan comes to public notice.

1985 A year-long miners' strike is brought to an end.
Mikhail Gorbachov succeeds Chernenko as Soviet leader.
Football riot at the Heysel Stadium in Brussels kills 34 people.
President Reagan and Mr Gorbachov hold their first Summit meeting.

1986 "Baby Doc" Duvalier deposed as President of Haiti.
Assassination of Mr Olaf Palme, Prime Minister of Sweden.
Challenger space shuttle explodes in flight, killing seven astronauts.
President Marcos replaced by Mrs Cory Aquino as President of the Philippines.

1987 200 die as the ferry *Herald of Free Enterprise* capsizes at Zeebrugge.
"Arms to Iran" enquiry takes place in Washington.
Margaret Thatcher returned to power for a third consecutive term.